Roz Stirling's *Breakfast with God* is all about
fresh to you. Feed on it and it will nourish
satisfy you, delight you and make you hung

Fresh, immediate, in-yer-face, like OJ with the bits in, *Breakfast with God* is a really good starter for your day. It's life-related and written by someone who knows what it's like to try to be a Christian in hard places. Read the Bible this way – it'll do you good.

Breakfast with God will refresh the parts other Bible reading guides cannot reach! It's creative, stimulating material. It's an insightful and pithy treatment of both familiar and unfamiliar passages. It will help any reader mine nuggets of wisdom from God's word for today's world.

Also available from HarperCollins*Publishers:*

Breakfast with God Volume 1 Duncan Banks
Breakfast with God Volume 2 Gerard Kelly

Breakfast with God

Volume 3

Roz Stirling

Marshall Pickering
An Imprint of HarperCollins*Publishers*

Marshall Pickering is an Imprint of
HarperCollins*Religious*
part of HarperCollins*Publishers*
77-85 Fulham Palace Road, London W6 8JB
www.christian-publishing.com

First published in Great Britain in 2000 by Marshall Pickering

1 3 5 7 9 10 8 6 4 2

Scripture quotations marked NIV are taken from the *Holy Bible, New International Version*,
© 1873, 1978, 1984 by International Bible Society. Used by permission of Hodder & Stoughton
Ltd, a member of the Hodder Headline Plc Group. All rights reserved. 'NIV' is a trademark of
International Bible Society. UK trademark number 1448790.

Scripture quotations marked NCV are taken from *The Youth Bible, New Century Version*
(Anglicized Edition) copyright © 1993 by Nelson Word Ltd, 501 Nelson Place, PO Box 141000,
Nashville TN 37214-1000, USA.

A catalogue record for this book is available from the British Library.

ISBN 0 551 03260 X

Printed and bound in Great Britain by
Martins the Printers Ltd,
Berwick upon Tweed

*This book is dedicated to
Patrick, Claire, Marc, Michael, Josh and Arianna,
and the young people of their generation.*

ACKNOWLEDGEMENTS

With special thanks to Trevor Morrow and William Crawley for their helpful insights, to the wonderful team in the Youth Office for their expert word processing and the many young people whose stories are the reason this book was written.

INTRODUCTION

The Bible is the world's best seller. No doubt about it. It ranks number one and has done for some time. You should make sure you don't miss out on this classic, not because it's a bestseller. No, that would be missing the point. Get into this great book because nothing is more important, nothing more urgent than meeting the author. The Bible is his story, his way of making sure you get a clear picture of who he is and how important you are to him. The Bible is his special way of revealing himself to you and anyone else who will take the time to read his book. God had you and I in mind when he left the Bible for us. He wants us to read it as often as we can. He wants us to discover that it has an endless supply of insights, instruction, encouragement, challenge and direction for living our lives. Get into the Bible today.

Breakfast with God will help you get started. Make it part of your wake-up programme. Read a BWG every morning with your brekkie. That will get you reading the Bible every day in a way that helps you think about its message for you and the things God wants you to remember or to do for him. He will be delighted that you want to spend this time with him. But hey, don't get all hung up if you miss a day. God isn't looking for a rigid workout schedule. He's looking for a great relationship with you. A friendship that works in both directions. So do the best you can with your time schedule and if you're not a morning person then pick up the story at lunchtime or settle in at bedtime and have that special time when just you and God get to be alone.

Breakfast with God will open up the story for you and help you get to know this great author. He's waiting to meet you so go for it – now!

Orange Juice

But the angel said to him: 'Do not be afraid, Zechariah; your prayer has been heard. Your wife Elizabeth will bear you a son, and you are to give him the name John.'

LUKE 1:13 NIV

A TURN UP FOR THE BOOKS

The Big Breakfast

Have you ever been to Disney World? You know the score: the faster the ride, the steeper the drop! You thought you knew what you were letting yourself in for, but oh boy, that was really something. It was… well, how *do* you describe it? You can't. It scared you half to death. It made you laugh and cry all at the same time.

Well, an angel called Gabriel showed up at the temple. He appeared to an old man – and scared *him* half to death! It was Zechariah the priest, who had prayed to God for years and years, asking God to send the Messiah. You see, God had promised he would send a messiah – a saviour – for the Jews, God's own people, but many of them had given up waiting. God had kind of gone out of their lives for about 400 years, and now here they were, living like prisoners in their own country, under the rule of a foreign power. But what has Zechariah's promised son John got to do with the Messiah?

Continental

John was sent by God to prepare the way. He was sent to get people ready for the awesome appearance of their Messiah – God himself in human skin and bone!

Coffee

When God makes a promise, he always keeps it – but his timing is often a challenge to our faith. Don't ever give up on him.

Orange Juice

For to us a child is born, to us a son is given… And he will be called Wonderful Counsellor, Mighty God, Everlasting Father, Prince of Peace.

ISAIAH 9:6 NIV

HEAR YE... HEAR YE...

The Big Breakfast

Christmas brings out the kid in us. There's just something about it: parties and presents; great food and super TV; oh, and those carols about the baby Jesus in the manger. I always look forward to Christmas. But where does the baby Jesus story fit in with the rest of it?

Well, in some ways it doesn't. Mind you, God loves a party and he gives great presents. But those aren't the important bits. Isaiah tells us what it's really about: God, the Almighty, coming to earth as a baby. Imagine!

'Hold on,' you say. 'Isaiah wrote his book long before Jesus arrived in that stable!' Well, yes he did. So what we have here is God making an announcement. The incredible bit is that God gives this news at a time when people were so afraid of him, so in awe of him, that they were scared even to use his name. So to be told that God would become like them and would be born to a human mum and dad was mind-blowing!

Continental

What is the most amazing thing that has ever happened to you? Now multiply that by a thousand million – and you still aren't close to the incarnation!

Coffee

Don't allow the Christian story to become so familiar that it seems ordinary. Instead stop, look, listen and then worship with all your heart.

Orange Juice

A record of the genealogy of Jesus Christ, the son of David, the son of Abraham…

MATTHEW 1:1 NIV

DNA

The Big Breakfast

So it's all to do with DNA, is it? Supermodel Cindy Crawford was asked in an interview what the secret of her success was, and she replied, 'Genetic luck.' What about that? It was all made for her before she was born. She has a point.

I bet you've never read this genealogy thing in Matthew chapter 1. It's just a long list of names after all, and while there are a few people you would recognize, you've certainly never heard of the rest. In fact, you can't even pronounce their names. What was Matthew thinking about, putting that long, boring list at the start of his book?

Well, for one thing, all those names tell us something about people from one generation to the next who made mistakes, told lies, slept with other people's wives, even killed one another.

The reason for Matthew's long list was to let us have a look at the 'genetic luck' that Jesus was going to have. These people were all his ancestors.

Another reason for Matthew's long list was to make sure we knew that Jesus was born Jewish.

Continental

The royal line of the King of Kings makes for some interesting reading, don't you think? Why did God allow this?

Coffee

God wanted to get as close as possible to us, yet stay uniquely God. Impossible? Think about it. It's the most awesome event ever to take place.

Orange Juice

God sent the angel Gabriel to Nazareth… to a virgin… Mary… the angel said to her, '…You will be with child and give birth to a son…'

LUKE 1:26-31 NIV

YOU'VE BEEN BEEPED!

The Big Breakfast

Have you seen the movie *City of Angels?* Seth the angel exists in Los Angeles. He and his mates have a big job, watching over the whole of LA. Their main thing is being there when someone is ready to pass to the other side. Seth is doing his regular job when he sees Maggie for the first time. Now the story really begins. I'll leave you to watch the movie to catch the rest.

There's a great line in it that I loved: 'You've been beeped.' Seth is talking to Maggie, who hasn't quite grasped the fact that he's an angel. 'You've been beeped. The angel has spoken to you, Maggie.'

Well, in the passage quoted above, Mary has been beeped! Gabriel is back, this time to talk to a girl. The news is disturbing. She's going to have a baby.

Stop for a moment. Disturbing? Yes, this girl hasn't slept with anyone. Now she's been told she's going to be a mother – of God, no less! What's going on? Has this particular angel been on the job too long today?

Continental

Mary knew that Gabriel was 'all there'. He had his message straight. Just look at Mary's courageous answer (v. 38): 'I am the Lord's servant… May it be to me as you have said.'

Coffee

If God came to you and asked you to accept a challenge as big as this one, what would you do? Mary was a girl with her own plans for her life, just like you.

Orange Juice
He has helped his servant Israel, remembering to be merciful to Abraham and his descendants for ever, even as he said to our fathers.

LUKE 1:54–55 NIV

A SONG FOR THE WHOLE WORLD

The Big Breakfast
You're at a party. Imagine you've just been told the solution to one of those irritating puzzles, the kind of thing that usually keeps you baffled for hours. Now you've been given the answer, and of course it's so obvious, so simple. You laugh to yourself as others who aren't in the know come up with a billion complicated solutions to solve the riddle.

This verse in Luke 1 is a bit of a riddle too. Until, that is, you get the inside story. This is part of Mary's song, the one she sang to Elizabeth. Who's Elizabeth? She's the mother of John. Mary and Elizabeth were celebrating the fact that Mary was pregnant. How strange. In those days an unmarried, pregnant girl was a disgrace, not a blessing.

They were celebrating, though, because they understood the riddle. It was easy to solve if you had faith! They had faith. They knew their Bible. Isaiah 7:14 told them that the Messiah would be born to a virgin. Mary was that virgin.

Continental
Our lives, and the things that happen to us, can seem like a riddle that makes no sense. Until we look towards God, that is. He's committed to solving our riddles, putting things straight. Give him the opportunity to do just that.

Coffee
What faith challenges do you face at the moment? Learn from Mary. She was able to step out, to go for God because she knew him well through the Scriptures.

Orange Juice

Joseph, son of David, do not be afraid to take Mary home as your wife, because what is conceived in her is from the Holy Spirit.

MATTHEW 1:20 NIV

ZZZ...

The Big Breakfast

I don't know about you, but when I dream it's a wild and crazy mix of bizarre people and places. My dreams rarely make sense. I do remember one dream, though, that warned me not to do a certain thing. Somehow I just knew that dream was different.

Here we have Joseph, the fiancé of Mary. God is speaking to him in a dream, and what God is saying to Joseph is pretty heavy stuff. 'Don't be afraid to take Mary as your wife.' You want to protest with Joseph. 'But she's *pregnant*! Don't you understand, God? This baby isn't mine. I haven't slept with her! How could she do this to me?'

Put yourself in Joseph's shoes. He's a carpenter. He needs his reputation, so he has decided to break things off with Mary. Quietly, mind – he doesn't want to make things any more difficult than they are already. Then God shows up in his dream and tells him quite the opposite. Would you have the courage to believe God was speaking?

Continental

Morpheus: 'Have you ever had a dream, Neo, that you were so sure was real? What if you were unable to wake from that dream? How would you know the difference between the dream world and the real world?'
(From the movie *The Matrix*, 1999)
Did Joseph feel like this, I wonder?

Coffee

Think of the consequences for Mary and Joseph. They chose to believe. Has God called you to take him at his word? Do it.

Orange Juice

While they were there, the time came for the baby to be born, and she gave birth to her firstborn, a son.

LUKE 2:6-7 NIV

The Big Breakfast

Bill Clinton came to Belfast a while ago. The President of the United States. You just would not have believed it. Motorways were closed. No other vehicle could travel the route at the same time as the President. Trees were cut down so that he would never be out of sight. Men talking up their shirtsleeves were everywhere. Camera crews and TV networks from all over the world caught every moment of the visit and beamed it around the world. What a commotion. Nobody, absolutely nobody, missed it.

The Lord of the Universe, the King of Kings, was born in a smelly, urine-filled stable, to a teenage girl who was helped by a rough, and probably frightened, carpenter.

Take a second or two to picture this moment in history. God, who reduced himself to the size of a human foetus, allowed the manner of his coming to be unmajestic and extraordinarily humble. The world slept, but heaven was in uproar, with angels overcome by the work of the Mighty God.

Continental

The circumstances that surrounded the birth of Jesus were mind-blowing – a dangerous journey from Nazareth to Bethlehem, a filthy stable floor, an untrained midwife! Would you allow your baby to be born in such conditions?

Coffee

Think about the incredible humility of the Sovereign God, his determination to be like us. I want you to understand what it took for God to reach you. Yes, you. Has it sunk in? It's awesome. Don't waste such a gift.

Orange Juice
As Jesus was walking beside the Sea of Galilee, he saw two brothers…
'Come, follow me,' Jesus said.

MATTHEW 4:18–19 NIV

MAKE FOLLOWING WORTH IT!

The Big Breakfast
Some years back there was a man from the United States who tramped round the world with a huge wooden cross. He was called Arthur Blessit and he caused quite a stir. I remember him coming to our town. Everyone was talking about him. Loads of people turned up to hear him speak. Some even began to travel with him. It was a bit like that scene in the movie *Forrest Gump*. Forrest was walking the world, and people fell in behind him and started walking with him. It was all a bit silly, really, but following is something we humans do. Take a look at the trainers you're wearing. Who started that fashion craze? Mr Nike? Now look how many of us are following it.

Jesus reaches out to the part of us that wants to follow, the part of us that gets excited about great causes. Jesus is the greatest cause of all. Follow him and you will find yourself in a relationship that makes the hike worth it.

Continental
Jesus has a load of competition these days. Voice after voice yells at us every day: 'Buy me!' 'Love me!' 'Indulge me!' Be smart enough to follow Jesus *all* the way, not just part of it.

Coffee
I have been a Christian for many years. I think the most important thing I've learned is that following Jesus is often a struggle, but it's always the best road.

Orange Juice
After that, he poured water into a basin and began to wash his disciples' feet.

JOHN 13:5 NIV

GOD ON THE DOLE

The Big Breakfast
I was one of those people who left college and went straight into my first teaching job. After a few years I left and took up work with a charity. It was a short-term contract and three years later I found myself on the dole. I will never forget the experience of those few months. To get into the system, I had to go through the humiliation of answering a load of personal questions, which were put to me by a girl I had once taught. She never once lifted her eyes from the page. The next ordeal was the weekly dole queue. There was another past pupil at the counter. I felt like a piece of discarded rubbish.

One day I looked back down the queue. There was someone I recognized. What was he doing here? It was the headmaster of the school where I had taught. I felt so embarrassed for him. How was he going to feel when he got to the counter?

This verse reminds me of a situation like that. Instead of God peering at us from behind the glass screen, he is in the queue with us.

Continental
There is no position lower than that of a servant. Yet that is how far down Jesus chose to go.

Coffee
Who do you need to serve today? No matter how difficult it is for you, do it. It will change your life.

Orange Juice

Love must be sincere. Hate what is evil; cling to what is good. Be devoted to one another in brotherly love. Honour one another above yourselves.

ROMANS 12:9-10 NIV

NO FAKERY

The Big Breakfast

I read the following letter on an agony page of a magazine recently.

> My boyfriend says he loves me, but he has trouble showing it. I always do special things for him, like sending him surprise love letters, but he only does nice things for me when I complain that he is not expressing his feelings. He says he is just very laid back and that he's never felt about another girl the way he feels about me.

How are you doing on the 'expressing your feelings' front? Do your friends and those special people in your life know that they are loved?

Jesus has a great plan for the people who get into his type of love. It's a love that isn't afraid to be real, that doesn't need to be prompted to show up. It's about being devoted to one another – caring so much about one another that somebody else always comes first. Now that's the kind of love I want to experience.

Continental

Whenever I talk to people who have no time for church, I'm always interested to discover how fascinated they are with religion. Everybody wants some kind of spiritual reality. Is this a search for real love?

Coffee

This lovely verse tells us what people in church are like. Do you recognize anyone?

Orange Juice

Bless those who persecute you; bless and do not curse. Rejoice with those who rejoice; mourn with those who mourn.

ROMANS 12:14–15 NIV

ROBBEN ISLAND

The Big Breakfast

'Mummy, Mummy, I've done it! I've got the part. They're going to let me play Nora, the leading role. I can't believe it! And that gorgeous Nick will play my oppressive, controlling husband. I'm over the moon!' It will be easy for this mother to rejoice with her girl. It's her daughter's first big part, and she plans to go to drama school.

'Rejoice with those who rejoice.' Sure, I can do that. Well, most people can. 'Bless those who persecute you.' Hmm. If you're anything like me, you will fume and puff and plan a tactical revenge – and that's only for minor persecutions. Bless? Not on your life.

Then there's the serious stuff, when someone is really out to get you – the kind of thing that's about destroying you or some part of you. The Bible makes it clear. Our job as Christians is to bless. To return good for evil. To find ways of doing good to those who mean to harm us. This kind of response, while it is the obligation of every Christian, can only be done with the help of God's Spirit.

Continental

In his book *A Witness For Ever*, Michael Cassidy tells of the power of such a spirit-filled response. One ANC leader who had spent time on Robben Island with Nelson Mandela spoke of a moment when he took courage and reached out in friendship to a brutal and cruel warden. The warden was reduced to tears.

Coffee

Lord Jesus, your power to transform the most brutal, cruel person is still around today. Give me the courage to bless those who persecute me.

Orange Juice

I am the good shepherd. The good shepherd lays down his life for the sheep. The hired hand is not the shepherd...he abandons the sheep and runs away.

JOHN 10:11–12 NIV

CULTURAL MISFIT

The Big Breakfast

A few years ago, Ben Johnston of MTV was quoted as saying, 'We don't influence 11–14-year-olds, we own them already.' That's a pushy statement. I guess he was saying MTV have been so good that kids drink in every word. It's more than an influence. It's a bible. It tells us how to think, dress and behave. I get very bothered by that, because I know Ben Johnston is right.

Take a look at the magazines in the newsagents. Watch the TV soaps. Some of it's just a laugh, certainly, something to relax in front of in the evening. But look again. It's put together very carefully with you in mind. Well, maybe not you, but definitely the money you'll feed into it. It tunes into the issues that mess you up. It tells you what's cool, hip, exciting, what must be had at all costs. So you keep buying the magazines, you keep watching the TV. Do you want to be owned by Ben Johnston? I don't think so. As the American rock star Larry Norman sings: 'Why don't you look into Jesus, he's got the answer...'

Continental

There are two people in Jesus' story – the shepherd and the farm labourer. The shepherd has invested in these sheep, so he cares about them. Jesus has invested in you.

Coffee

'Don't become so well adjusted to your culture that you fit into it without even thinking. Instead fix your attention on God.' (From Romans 12, *The Message* by Eugene Peterson)

Orange Juice

Now one of the Pharisees invited Jesus to have dinner with him… When a woman who had lived a sinful life in that town learned that Jesus was eating at the Pharisee's house, she brought an alabaster jar of perfume.

LUKE 7:36–37 NIV

KETCHUP

The Big Breakfast

A friend of mine told me a wonderful story. He was in church, when halfway through the service a homeless man came in. The man was restless. He moved from seat to seat. Perhaps he was looking for a warm spot. He eventually settled down. A few people stole glances at him, but mostly he was ignored. Then he brought out his dinner. Fish and chips. The smell was distracting and the man was a noisy eater. An elder of the church got up to investigate. After a few minutes he left the man, walked to the front of the church and out through the door. He returned a few minutes later with a bottle of ketchup.

This verse in Luke 7 is about an unusual guest arriving at a dinner party. Like the homeless man, she stood out. She also took a great risk. The dinner party host had the power to have her stoned to death. She was a prostitute and death by stoning was often their fate. Why, then, did she come? Jesus was the reason.

Continental

Jesus is a very special man. People all around you need to meet him, but they don't realize it. They have often confused fame and the attention of a crowd as the reasons for Jesus' popularity. You need to show them the real Jesus.

Coffee

Jesus will be seen more easily when those of us who know him learn how to fetch the ketchup!

Orange Juice

…and as she stood behind him at his feet weeping, she began to wet his feet with her tears.

LUKE 7:38A NIV

FRIENDS

The Big Breakfast

Do you enjoy the comedy show *Friends*? Everyone seems to be into it. A recent poll of teenagers had it at the top of the list of favourite shows. I just love Chandler. He's my favourite, with great lines like, 'Did they teach you that in your anger management class?' The great theme of *Friends*, though, is in the song. 'I'll be there for you…' Isn't that what friendship's all about?

We are in a story here about Jesus coming for dinner. Was he at a friend's house? It doesn't look like it, because some of the usual, nice things about being at a friend's house are missing. No one offers to wash his feet. He doesn't get the kind of greeting you'd give a friend.

Then this woman shows up. *She* does all the things that were missing. She washes Jesus' feet with tears, and dries them with her hair. What was this all about?

Well, seems to me it was about showing gratitude and love to someone who had been a real friend to her. Jesus was her friend.

Continental

'I'll be there for you.' Can you say that about your friends? Do you care for them that much? Do you invest in their lives and put yourself out on their behalf?

Coffee

Take time today to think about your friends and how much you do for them. Then choose three of them and plan something that will make them feel special and loved.

Orange Juice
Then she wiped them with her hair, kissed them and poured perfume on them.

LUKE 7:38B NIV

NETIQUETTE

The Big Breakfast
There is a cracking word being bandied about in the computer world – 'netiquette'. Everything has a right and a wrong way of being done, even in the world of IT.

What are the things that help you fit in? The right language? The right gear? Being great at football? Every generation has them, you know. When I was a teenager one of the big things was platform boots. There's nothing wrong with platform boots, of course, except that you can't walk in them.

This woman who has turned up at the dinner party doesn't care what people think of her. She isn't much into what will make her fit. She has found a new way to belong and it beats everything. To get to it, however, she has to cross a few lines. Letting her hair down, for example, is a big deal: it just wasn't done by women in public in those days. What makes it worse is that she could be making things difficult for Jesus. Jesus isn't getting all hot and bothered, though. He knows what's going on.

Continental
Has Jesus become so familiar, so domestic, that we just don't understand this woman's behaviour? She was all eaten up with love for him. 'Netiquette' was out of the window.

Coffee
I want you to get so excited about Jesus, so caught up by who he is and how much he loves you, that you don't care what your friends think. Ask him to help you.

Orange Juice

When the Pharisee who invited him saw this, he said to himself, 'If this man were a prophet, he would know who is touching him…'

LUKE 7:39 NIV

GOD DON'T MAKE JUNK

The Big Breakfast

God spoke with an accent. Have you ever thought about that? Jesus' home district, perhaps even the town of Nazareth that he came from, would have been identified immediately by those who heard him speak, because of his accent.

He was a Galilean. That meant Jesus was judged by some as a person of low position. He had a 'common' accent. It gave away the fact that he was a very ordinary man. So what was all this talk about him being a prophet? Simon and the other religious leaders had decided it was impossible for a prophet to come from such common roots.

God may not have called you to be a prophet, but he has called you to be his child and that gives you enormous value. Don't ever believe you're a nobody, or that you're second-rate. There is no second-rate with God. Whatever your background, whatever your accent, you are very special. God has made sure of that by sending Jesus to die for you.

Continental

A kid from the New York Bronx wrote the following words on a card and set it on his desk: 'I'm me, and I'm okay, 'cause God don't make junk!'

Coffee

Accept yourself today for who you are. Don't measure yourself by other people or what they expect of you. 'God don't make junk', so feel special today. God thinks you are.

Orange Juice

If this man were a prophet, he would know who is touching him and what kind of woman she is – that she is a sinner.

LUKE 7:39 NIV

FREE YOUR MIND

The Big Breakfast

Here is a great line from the movie *The Matrix*. Morpheus says to Neo, 'I'm trying to free your mind, Neo, but I can only show you the door. You're the one that has to walk through it.' There's something about that line that fits with this verse from Luke 7. Jesus is trying very hard to free a lot of people's minds. The man called Simon, who leads the 'God squad' group at the dinner party, is making all sorts of mistakes in the conclusions he reaches. Jesus wants to free his mind.

First he has decided that Jesus can't be a prophet because of his accent. Now he has decided that Jesus is a naïve fool who doesn't understand that the woman who has wet his feet with her tears is a prostitute. For Simon that's another sign that Jesus is only an ordinary guy.

Oh dear, Simon. You just keep getting it wrong. Not only is Jesus fully aware of the woman's status, but he can read your heart too.

Continental

The only way we will ever understand things from God's perspective is for us to set aside our own smart answers and listen out for his.

Coffee

Have you ever made a completely wrong judgement yet been convinced that you were right? Ask God to help you be ready to admit that you're wrong – if you are.

Orange Juice

Two men owed money to a certain money-lender. One owed him 500 denarii, and the other 50. Neither of them had the money to pay him back, so he cancelled the debts of both. Now which of them will love him more?

LUKE 7:41–42 NIV

DROP THE DEBT

The Big Breakfast

Everybody should know about it: the campaign to drop the debt. Many developing countries are crippled by the massive interest payments they make every year to the developed countries. They are in trouble, though. They haven't enough revenue to pay the interest, never mind the money they owe. Meanwhile, their country's development doesn't happen. Education, health and industrial development are all held back. The campaign by a number of Christian charities to have the debt dropped, the slate wiped clean, has been quite successful. Governments have taken notice. Some of the debt has been dropped.

Jesus is telling a story here. It has a clear message about dropping debt. He tells the story to challenge the ungenerous heart of Simon, his host. Simon has watched the actions of a woman who knew she had done wrong, who also knew she had been forgiven and was now responding with gratitude. Simon missed this point altogether.

We are often unable to believe that the gift of God's forgiveness to us is a cancelled debt – just like the story; just like the deal with the developing countries. I wonder why?

Continental

Nothing we do can make God love us more. Nothing we do can make him love us less. He made his mind up about us before we were born.

Coffee

Do you sometimes privately wonder if you really need God's forgiveness as much as other people? Ask God to show you your heart.

Orange Juice

Two men owed money to a certain money-lender… Now which of them will love him more?

LUKE 7:41–42 NIV

WHAT'S LOVE GOT TO DO WITH IT?

The Big Breakfast

I happen to think that Tina Turner is fantastic. She has such energy, passion and style. And her song 'What's love got to do with it?' is great.

What is love? How do we define love? How do we measure it? What does it look like? Sometimes, when somebody says 'I love you', they really mean 'I need you' or 'I can't cope without you'. They're really talking about themselves. I've been quite sickened by some of the celebrity love tangles we've seen in the papers and gossip magazines. If somebody wants a particular partner, they seem to use all their celebrity influence to get hold of them, and they say they did it in the name of love! This isn't love. This is selfishness.

Love is a decision – a decision to invest in another person's life, to help them get the best out of everything, to give them time, energy and compassion; a decision to stick with them through the tough spots, to learn to say 'I'm sorry' and start again. If you were loved like this, you would feel very special. This is how God loves us.

Continental

When we're loved – truly loved – by someone, it's a great gift. We usually return the gift, but initially we must accept it.

Coffee

Lord, I've become so familiar with the idea that you love me that I take it and you for granted. I'm sorry.

Orange Juice

Simon replied, 'I suppose the one who had the bigger debt cancelled.' 'You have judged correctly,' Jesus said.

LUKE 7:43 NIV

LOOK IN THE MIRROR

The Big Breakfast

Have you seen the movie *Erin Brockovich*? Julia Roberts is great in the lead role. Erin has fought a legal battle against a big corporation on behalf of a local community. A factory next door has contaminated the water supply and people and their families have become very sick. It's the usual story, though: the corporation is working on a cover-up. The case goes to court. A staggering $333 million is awarded, the largest such payout in American history (this movie is based on a true story). There is a very moving scene towards the end. Erin is telling one of the residents that they've won, and how much they've won. You need your hankie. Overcome, the resident really doesn't know how to thank Erin.

Let's go back to Jesus and his host. Jesus' story has exposed Simon's ungracious heart. Now Jesus has forced Simon to see that he and the prostitute are equal, because they are both in debt to God. They both need his forgiveness. It doesn't matter what size the debt is. The more aware you are of your debt, the easier it will be to be grateful.

Continental

When you judge yourself to be better than someone else, watch out. Like Simon, you might discover that you are the one with whom God has the bigger problem.

Coffee

Lord, my natural tendency is to see others' faults more easily than my own. Help me to look honestly at myself and recognize good in others.

Orange Juice

Then he turned towards the woman and said to Simon, 'Do you see this woman? I came into your house. You did not give me any water for my feet…'

LUKE 7:44A NIV

ADD SOME JEWELLERY

The Big Breakfast

Who will ever forget that television shot from years back of Diana, Princess of Wales, reaching out to grasp the hand of a man dying from AIDS? This was at a time when we were scared of AIDS, and all sorts of rumours were flying around about how it was passed on. When the Princess touched this sick man, it was a precious thing. She might as well have given him the crown jewels.

When Jesus turned towards the woman and spoke of her in that public gathering, he placed a diamond necklace around her neck. She was an outcast; Simon was a respected community leader. Jesus was breaking two rules: he was attacking Simon for being a poor host, and he was giving dignity to a woman known to be a prostitute. Neither was an acceptable thing to do. But then, Jesus wasn't into keeping the self-important people happy. He was much more concerned about the things that God thought were important.

Continental

Human rights and dignity are important. We all realize that these days. Yet still we walk past the man sleeping in a doorway as if he were invisible.

Coffee

Lord, give me the courage to challenge anything in my society that takes dignity away from another human being. Give me your eyes and your courage.

Orange Juice

Do you see this woman? I came into your house. You did not give me any water for my feet, but she wet my feet with her tears and wiped them with her hair.

LUKE 7:44 NIV

HILLARY FOR PRESIDENT

The Big Breakfast

Can you imagine Hillary Clinton as President of the United States instead of her husband? It might happen someday.

Women have had a hard fight to get recognition and be offered important jobs or positions. Look around you. What do you see? Do you see only equality, where it's appropriate – or is there still a bias towards the men?

God made the sexes with some very special roles in mind. It's a masterplan. For some roles or tasks either a man or a woman would be appropriate. Others are the special privilege of either the man or the woman.

Jesus didn't like it when he saw God's design being wrecked. He was around at a time when women were considered second-rate. There was even a prayer the men said which thanked God that they weren't women! Jesus doesn't tolerate such an attitude. His actions here and elsewhere in Scripture give enormous dignity to women, challenging yet another social injustice.

Continental

Once you have grasped the extent to which women were oppressed in this culture, the dignity Jesus publicly gave to them is staggering.

Coffee

Take a moment to consider the upheaval Jesus caused. He didn't allow things to pass if they were wrong. As his follower, what kind of impact are you making?

Orange Juice

You did not give me a kiss, but this woman, from the time I entered, has not stopped kissing my feet. You did not put oil on my head, but she has poured perfume on my feet.

LUKE 7:45–46 NIV

UNDER YOUR SKIN

The Big Breakfast

I once worked with a woman who really knew how to get under my skin. I imagined that she sat at home thinking about her tactics, because the shots always seemed to come from behind. She had the precision of a long-range missile. The problem for me was that I didn't know what I'd done to upset her. I presumed it was something to do with the job I'd got, but that was only a guess. Whether or not her actions were intentional, she certainly managed to get below the surface nearly every day.

I reckon that Jesus knew he was getting under Simon's skin. He was trying to. It was not because he wanted to put Simon down or intentionally make a fool of him, but rather because he wanted Simon to do a bit of self-examination, to take an honest and careful look at himself.

Simon, however, seemed to have no real awareness of where he was getting it wrong.

Continental

We all have something of Simon in us, when we get a bit frosty towards God because we reckon we can run things pretty well for ourselves.

Coffee

God doesn't want us to turn in on ourselves, to search our every tiny wrongdoing – but he does want us to be honest about the overall picture.

Orange Juice

Therefore, I tell you, her many sins have been forgiven – for she loved much. But he who has been forgiven little loves little.

LUKE 7:47 NIV

MISSING THE POINT

The Big Breakfast

What do you think it was like, being around when Jesus was here, listening to him challenge the establishment or tell one of those strange stories that didn't seem to make sense? You have to hand it to him: he had guts. He certainly was a man with a mission.

I wonder what it would have felt like when he told this woman that her sins were forgiven? He won't have sounded like one of those wacky religious freaks who manipulate people into following them. No. Jesus, I'm sure, would have been self-assured but not arrogant, at one with himself, even though some people around him were gasping in horror.

We've missed the point, though. Jesus didn't actually forgive the woman's sins there on the spot. What Jesus did was to point out that the woman, because she was sorry, had allowed herself to receive the forgiveness that was *already* waiting for her. Simon, of course, had missed this point all along, because of his hostility towards Jesus.

Continental

It's important to catch what Jesus is saying to the woman herself. This woman was drawn into love for Jesus *because she was forgiven*. She wasn't trying to earn her forgiveness.

Coffee

Look around you today at your friends and colleagues who don't know Jesus. Are you praying for them, that they might catch sight of the real Jesus?

Orange Juice

Then Jesus said to her, 'Your sins are forgiven.'

LUKE 7:48 NIV

The Big Breakfast

What must Jesus' words have felt like for this woman? What he said was simple, direct and to the point. It wasn't a case of telling her to sign up for a class and we'll see if you can graduate. No, it was simple: 'Your sins are forgiven.'

When Jesus comes to us today it's still dead simple. Tell him where you've messed up, bring it to him, say sorry and give him the right to call the shots. You'll hear the same message: 'Your sins are forgiven.'

I used to work with tough kids from the inner city. Life for them had been lived by the law of the jungle – he who got the first punch in survived. The rules were made up from moment to moment. One golden rule was that you never admitted you'd got it wrong. That was to be weak, to be out of control and easy prey. Coming to Jesus and saying sorry for getting things wrong was a huge leap for these young people. It didn't need to be. Saying sorry to Jesus is not a sign of weakness but of great strength.

Continental

'I believe God wants me to quit concentrating on myself and on my own agenda and instead focus on him. He wants me to keep it simple.' (Jim Aitkins, Youth Pastor from Washington)

Coffee

Lord Jesus, thank you for your wonderful invitation to love you and follow you. I accept.

Orange Juice
The other guests began to say among themselves, 'Who is this who even forgives sins?'

LUKE 7:49 NIV

WHO IS THIS GUY?

The Big Breakfast
The guests are horrified! They, like Simon, had come to this banquet to test Jesus. Was he or was he not a prophet, or even 'the prophet', the Messiah? Then this woman comes in and behaves in the most inappropriate way. They've never seen the like. And now Jesus is applauding her, telling her what a great thing she's done and – horror of horrors – he's telling her that her sins are forgiven. To add insult to injury, he has also publicly humiliated his host and inferred that he, Simon the Pharisee, is the real sinner, not the woman!

Perhaps if you'd been this woman you would have found it easy to fall at Jesus' feet and declare your change of heart. How else was she to get public recognition for a new start? The Pharisees weren't going to give it to her. It was well known that she was a disreputable woman. Jesus was her only hope. Can you blame the guests, therefore, for their hostility towards the young teacher?

Continental
As he was offering God's forgiveness to this woman, Jesus knew that he had yet to demonstrate his enormous love through his death on the cross.

Coffee
What do you make of Jesus' death on the cross? Has our society become so sophisticated that we can't conceive of it as a relevant part of spirituality?

Orange Juice
Jesus said to the woman, 'Your faith has saved you; go in peace.'

LUKE 7:50 NIV

SPIRITUAL IS SOMETHING WE BECOME

The Big Breakfast
What makes for a good life? TV soaps tell us that sex is the road to all that's good: life begins because of sex; childhood and adolescence are all about discovering it; being an adult is about getting as much of it as you can. So sex must save the world, right?

Well, if it's not sex, what is it? Climbing the corporate ladder? Acquiring a bigger and better car, house, family? Oh, not that either – although you may only admit that quietly, when you're by yourself in the loo.

Having a good job is not something to be knocked. They're hard to find, and even harder to keep. Getting on well is okay too, as long as it doesn't demand every second of every day to stay there. And sex, well that's a pretty good thing as well, let's be honest.

None of it, though, is enough on its own. We need a relationship with God. Everybody is on a spiritual search these days. Jesus has proved so often that he is the one we're searching for.

Continental
During the 1950s, '60s and '70s, they tried to kill faith in God in many Eastern European countries. They couldn't. Faith is a gift from God.

Coffee
We're all seeking spiritual experience today. Faith in God and Jesus will take us way beyond mere experience and into a relationship. Pass that good news on.

Orange Juice
Hear, O LORD, and answer me, for I am poor and needy. Guard my life, for I am devoted to you…

PSALM 86:1-2A NIV

GUARD MY LIFE

The Big Breakfast
Where do you go when there's trouble in your life? Perhaps a better question to ask is *who* do you go to? Is it God? 'Of course I go to God,' I hear you say. At least, that's the theory.

The truth is, we're not very good at trusting God when things go wrong. Suddenly he seems very far away, and pretty hard to get close to. 'Was he ever there in the first place?' we begin to ask ourselves. Then those irritating doubts creep in.

We may not question his existence, but we do get mad at him. 'Why has he allowed this to happen to me?' We feel let down. It seems so unfair. You've been living the Christian life as best you can, so why has this happened?

There may not be a clear reason for your trouble – circumstances that were beyond your control; someone else's bad decision which left you hurt; being in the wrong place at the wrong time. In this Psalm, David is in deep trouble. God still figures for him, despite that.

Continental
David's need is raw and desperate. He remains devoted to God nonetheless.

Coffee
When life gets tough, don't be tempted to blame God. This is Satan's favourite sidetrack.

Orange Juice
Guard my life, for I am devoted to you. You are my God; save your servant
who trusts in you.

PSALM 86:2 NIV

CONFIDENCE IN GOD

The Big Breakfast
Many times in the Psalms we see King David in
trouble. We know from reading his life story
in 1 and 2 Samuel that his troubles often came
through doing what God had asked him to do. Does that
seem strange? On other occasions, of course, he got into real
bother all by himself. The Bathsheba affair, for example, was
entirely his own fault.

Why didn't David give up? Why didn't he tell God to let
him off the hook? You can picture it. David had been called by
God as a young boy. He had accepted the call. Further down
the line, he spent years living as a fugitive, on the run from a
mad king. Is that what it means to be called by God? What
about that promise of 'abundant life'? Where is it now?

David is devoted to God because he's totally convinced
about God's commitment to him. That's his secret. His life is
clearly under threat. With awesome confidence, David appeals
to God. He trusts him.

Continental
Perhaps one reason
for David's rock-solid
confidence in God
can be found in their
history. Verse 13 of
Psalm 86 allows us to
see that God has
been there for him
before: 'For great is
your love towards
me; you have
delivered me from
the depths of the
grave.'

Coffee
Take time to think back over your life with God. Write down all the times when
he was there for you. You've got a history with God too.

Orange Juice
Bring joy to your servant, for to you, O LORD, I lift up my soul.

PSALM 86:4 NIV

JOY BEYOND CIRCUMSTANCES

The Big Breakfast
What a strange thing to say at this point in his life! David, as we have already discovered, is barely hanging in there. He's looking to God for help, trusting God to get him out of this particular hard spot. But joy? Who even thinks about joy when things are really tough? It would be enough simply to get through this awful time. That would be just great. Time enough *then* to think about the better things in life.

Perhaps David had already discovered something that God wants us all to know. Our lives will have good times and bad times. Our circumstances will sometimes bring us a lot of fun, a lot of joy, and even great happiness. If you fall in love, for example, and your love is returned, it's just brilliant – there's no feeling on earth quite like it. You think your heart will burst with sheer joy. This, though, is circumstantial joy.

David lifts his soul to God. That means the whole of his life. He knows that a relationship with God is what he needs. He knows it works above everything else.

Continental
The kind of joy that David is asking God for is much deeper than the happiness that comes through pleasant circumstances.

Coffee
We're very slow to make the discovery David had made. Life will throw hard stuff at us. That's a fact. Don't blame God, though – instead, trust him for the deep joy that these circumstances will bring to you.

Orange Juice
You are forgiving and good, O LORD, abounding in love to all who call to you.

PSALM 86:5 NIV

GET GOING WITH GOD

The Big Breakfast
Have you ever really, really messed up on something? Got it so badly wrong that you want to die with shame? The worst bit is knowing that your own stubbornness got you into this mess. You just had to do it your way.

Then there is our world. How did some of that get so messed up? Try listing the good stuff. Now do the same for the bad stuff. We both know which list will be the longer one! It's really all down to stubborn people who just have to do things their way. Nature and God himself have warned us. Giving God complete control, however, is a bit too scary. Somehow we need to hold on, to keep some of the control for ourselves.

We don't see this kind of holding back from God as sin, do we? As far as we're concerned, sin is killing someone, or sleeping with someone else's wife. But holding back from God is sin too.

Continental
The Psalms are full of verses like today's. God is patiently waiting for us to come to him, to direct things for us.

Coffee
Are you too proud to invite God to lead the charge in your life? Or are you perhaps too stupid? 'Lord, I'm sorry,' is the place to start. Then get going with God.

Orange Juice
In the day of my trouble I will call to you, for you will answer me.

PSALM 86:7 NIV

GOD WILL ANSWER

The Big Breakfast
Heidi Wichlinski, talking a while ago about being engaged to Formula One driver David Coulthard, was philosophical about the danger David is in every time he steps into his custom-built McLaren car. 'I try not to think about the danger… if something goes wrong, well, it's destiny.' I guess that's one way to survive. The other David, the one writing this Psalm, has opted instead for trusting God at such times.

David had many good reasons for trusting God. He had a long memory, for a start. God had always shown up when he needed him. Remember the David and Goliath story? The young shepherd boy, going out to fight the armour-plated giant. It was a crazy thing to do, but David won. We discover why in 1 Samuel 17:45. David said to Goliath, 'I come against you in the name of the LORD Almighty…' History had taught David to trust God, to go to him when the heat was on.

Another reason for David's rock-solid confidence in God was that he *knew* God – really knew him. When you know somebody properly, trust is easy.

Continental
This sort of talk sounds rather silly today. Nobody believes in God like that any more. Or do they?

Coffee
Whatever is happening in your life today, no matter how tough it is, God will help you sort it out – if you ask him.

Orange Juice
All the nations you have made will come and worship before you, O LORD; they will bring glory to your name.

PSALM 86:9 NIV

ARE YOU SHAKY?

The Big Breakfast
There were wars all over the place, and vast numbers of people who didn't believe in God, and natural disasters and political upheavals. We're surrounded by the same kind of situations today. This, then, is a pretty bold statement. 'All the nations will worship the Lord!' Has David got his head in the sand?

What David knew, by faith, was that one day everybody would worship God. The thing that troubles me is how little of David's passion we seem to have now. What makes it worse is that other believers do have passion. Take Islam, for example. Talk to any young believer: they are total believers, totally committed, working together for the world domination of Islam. Meanwhile, we Christians apologize for daring to believe! Satan is smart. He knows that he's on to a winner if he can make Christians a little shaky about believing in God.

Continental
The world will one day know that God is the only true and living God. Don't allow yourself to be convinced otherwise.

Coffee
Pray that God will increase your faith in him and your passion for him. The world needs Christians who are consumed with both.

Orange Juice

Teach me your way, O LORD, and I will walk in your truth; give me an undivided heart, that I may fear your name.

PSALM 86:11 NIV

TELL ME YOUR TRUTH...

The Big Breakfast

David is pretty clear about one thing. He knows how great God is, and he knows that without God's help he will get it wrong. He needs God to teach him constantly. He needs God to bring him back again and again to the words that are the truth.

I don't hear that word, 'truth', used very often these days, at least not in the way David is using it. David is talking about a truth that comes from God. However, the word on the street these days is this: 'Tell me your truth and I'll tell you mine.' The Manic Street Preachers used that as a title of a song. The Street Preachers aren't on their own. Today everybody seems to believe that things are only true if they feel true.

The Bible is very clear when it tells us to look to God for truth. He alone can help us see it. Here David asks God to teach him. 'Reveal the truth to me, Lord.'

Continental

What 'truth' is David looking for? I imagine he wants to know how God would like things done, and he's ready to follow that.

Coffee

Lord, I have to say it's very hard sometimes to know what's true and what isn't. Help me find your truth, and live by it.

Orange Juice

Teach me your way, O LORD, and I will walk in your truth; give me an undivided heart, that I may fear your name.

PSALM 86:11 NIV

AN UNDIVIDED HEART

The Big Breakfast

What is David talking about in the second half of this verse? An 'undivided heart'? What in the world is that?

David is clued into himself – that is, he knows he has two sides. One side of him longs for God, really loves him, and knows that God is good, kind and compassionate. This side of him knows that only in God will he discover how to live. David wants to follow that side of himself.

But he has another side too. This is the side that got him into trouble when he saw Bathsheba taking a bath. Just look how far he fell on that one: adultery, lies, deceit, murder. Yes, all of that. David knows himself. He isn't going to be fooled by anyone who tells him he's not a bad guy really!

'Give me an undivided heart.' These are the words of someone who really understands God and himself.

Continental

In Proverbs chapter 1 we are told, 'The fear of the LORD is the beginning of knowledge' (v. 7a). 'Fear' in this context does not mean terror – it means deep respect.

Coffee

Lord, I want to know myself properly, to know when to be happy about myself and when I'm off course. Like David, I want to have a heart that pleases you.

Orange Juice
The arrogant are attacking me, O God; a band of ruthless men seeks my life – men without regard for you.

PSALM 86:14 NIV

'ÜBER-CELEBRITY'

The Big Breakfast
I read an article in which Victoria Beckham, Posh Spice, was talking about life as an 'über-celebrity'. A what? Well, it means being up there in a stratosphere all of your own. Even Jennifer Aniston and Madonna don't quite make it, apparently.

There are many perks, but the downside of having reached these dizzy heights is that everybody – at least in your own country – has an opinion about you. You get hassle on the street and wild stories written about you in the press. Victoria talks at one point about her hatred of a particular TV presenter who, on a weekly basis, 'rips us to pieces'.

I wonder if David was experiencing this kind of personal attack when he wrote Psalm 86. It's more than likely. David was being hounded by a mad king who was determined to destroy him. There may have been different reasons for the attacks, but they had the same impact on David personally as on Victoria Beckham. We don't know what Victoria does to deal with it. David went to God.

Continental
Is someone or something attacking you right now, pushing you, and your faith, right to the wire? Go to God. Don't keep trying to work it out for yourself.

Coffee
Lord, if I'm honest, I hang on by my fingernails at times like these. Thank you for your strength which stops them from breaking.

Orange Juice
Give me a sign of your goodness, that my enemies may see it and be put to shame, for you, O LORD, have helped me and comforted me.

PSALM 86:17 NIV

THE SIGN OF LEO

The Big Breakfast
So what's going on now, David? What's happened to that confidence of yours? Why are you asking God for a sign?

Actually, the sign isn't for David's benefit at all. It's for others. It's for the people who don't believe in God, to let them see who God is. The thing is, these 'signs' are there all the time, even today.

Tony Blair, the British Prime Minister, became a father for the fourth time not so long ago. This was the first baby to be born to a serving Prime Minister in Britain for 150 years. The safe arrival of baby Leo was a sign of God's goodness, just as it is with the safe arrival of every newborn baby. God is there, and has been there all along. It's a sign of his goodness.

We're back to faith again. The signs get missed because God has been pushed out of the picture. In their spiritual search, people are looking in other directions these days. God *is* good, though. He keeps on demonstrating his love, even when we're not looking.

Continental
You don't acquire trust and confidence in God overnight. It often takes us to hit some hard spots before our vision clears and we see him as he really is.

Coffee
Pray for your friends today, that these wonderful 'signs' of God all around them might open their eyes to him, so that they see him as he really is.

Orange Juice

On one occasion an expert in the law stood up to test Jesus. 'Teacher,' he asked, 'what must I do to inherit eternal life?'

LUKE 10:25 NIV

QUESTION TIME

The Big Breakfast

A recent newspaper poll revealed that the top question people would put to God is 'Why are there so many wars?' I'm not sure if that would be my first question. I do have other questions I'd want to put to God.

That's the great thing about God. He's there to answer any question we need to put to him – the one that comes out of our confusion because we don't quite understand something that the Bible says, or the one that comes out of our pain: 'Why is my Mum dying this slow and painful death if you're a God of love?'

This verse in Luke 10 is the start of a dialogue between Jesus and a young man who was an expert in religion. Jesus is ready for his questions. 'What must I do to inherit eternal life?' has a bit more behind it than a simple inquiry about the afterlife, however. Actually, it's only the beginning of a great dialogue between Jesus and this young man. Read on.

Continental

The Bible is not a fix-it manual to which we can run for instant solutions. It's God's story, and tells how his story intersects with ours.

Coffee

Lord, I have a heap of questions for you. Help me hear your answers as I take time to read your story properly.

Orange Juice

On one occasion an expert in the law stood up to test Jesus. 'Teacher,' he asked, 'what must I do to inherit eternal life?'

LUKE 10:25 NIV

SMOKE AND MIRROR TRICKS

The Big Breakfast

A trip to the circus came about once a year when we were kids. A really good team from Russia brought their cavalcade to town. The act that always got me was when they made something look as if it had disappeared or moved all by itself. You knew what you'd seen was an illusion, but how did they do it? You'd been had: they'd out-clevered you.

The circus trickster will often use a mirror or smoke to create his illusion. The first throws the image across the room so the object seems to have moved. The second hides the object so it seems to have disappeared.

The young man in Luke 10 is really hiding behind his question. It's a smoke screen. He's testing Jesus, trying to catch him out. Jesus, on the other hand, is holding up a mirror. He replies with another question (v. 26), and that question will show the young man his true reflection, his heart. That is what always matters to Jesus.

Continental

Jesus isn't trying to out-clever us with the challenges he gives us. He's trying to get us to see things as he sees them.

Coffee

Lord Jesus, your words are a mirror before me also. Help me to look into it and do something about what I see there.

Orange Juice
'What is written in the Law?' he replied. 'How do you read it?'

LUKE 10:26 NIV

NIT-PICKERS

The Big Breakfast
The question about eternal life was well chosen. It kicked off a lively debate. The religious guys of Jesus' day were nit-pickers. You know what that's like. They were people who paid way too much attention to petty details. They had even reduced the path to eternal life to a requirement to keep a load of petty rules. When Jesus asks the young man for a picture from the Bible about eternal life, he comes back at him with another quote (v. 27), this time from Leviticus and Deuteronomy. He quotes commandments that would be pretty tough for anyone to live out. Why did he choose these words?

Think about it. Jesus himself quoted these words about loving God in Mark 12. No commandment is greater than this, Jesus said. What was this young man up to? Was he trying to prove how well he knew his Bible? I don't think so. More likely, he was justifying how he lived already. 'Look, Jesus, I'm keeping the commandments. I'm okay.'

Continental
We can fall into this trap too – thinking the Christian faith is all about the way we do things. For Jesus, though, it all begins with our hearts.

Coffee
Lord Jesus, your gaze goes right through me. You always see what's in my heart. Help me to open myself to you and your love.

Orange Juice

He answered: ' "Love the Lord your God with all your heart and with all your soul and with all your strength and with all your mind"; and, "Love your neighbour as yourself." '

LUKE 10:27 NIV

HEART SURGERY

The Big Breakfast

Have you ever tried to lose weight? Most of us girls have. I know guys are weight-watchers too, but it's a girly thing to talk about it! It's a real grind. Unless you're one of those naturally disciplined people, you'll lose a few pounds, put them on again, then lose them again. Maybe for something special you might stick with the low-fat routine for long enough to make a real difference.

Loving God with all our heart is a good deal more important than losing weight. In fact, it's the essence of what being a Christian is all about. Yet on our own, by our own effort, to love God like this is impossible. We may reckon we love God like this, when something good happens, but unfortunately we get cold again very quickly. We need a bit of spiritual heart surgery to be able to give God the love he's really longing for. When we invite Jesus to journey with us, to stop us in our tracks and deal with the me-centred stuff, then this kind of love for God and our neighbour can grow.

Continental

The order Jesus gives us – of loving God and then our neighbour – is important. Our inner spirituality, the heart stuff, will show itself in how we treat others.

Coffee

Who is your neighbour? Your neighbour is anyone you meet. When we let God perform heart surgery on us, we find we care for that neighbour deeply.

Orange Juice

' "Love the Lord your God" ... "Love your neighbour as yourself." ' "You have answered correctly," Jesus replied.

LUKE 10:27-28A NIV

LIVE OUT THE ANSWER

The Big Breakfast

Jesus is responding here to that young man, the religious expert, who was trying to catch him out. Jesus wasn't worried about the games that were being played, or the attempts to trip him up. He loved that young man. He wanted him to see the depth of what loving God with all his heart would mean, the freedom it would bring to his life. Instead of following a rule-book religion, he could know a religion of the heart. He had answered Jesus' question correctly by talking about loving God with all his heart. The trouble was, he hadn't understood his own answer. He hadn't understood that living out the commandment could change his life. Jesus wanted him to experience that real change of life, and not simply stay within his religious comfort zone.

Continental

Although we need Jesus to do some heart surgery on us so that we can love God and others properly, he usually waits for us to ask him.

Coffee

Lord Jesus, I don't always understand how to live out the answer. Please help me. Please fill me with your love, both for you and for other people.

Orange Juice
'You have answered correctly,' Jesus replied. 'Do this and you will live.' But…

LUKE 10:28-29A NIV

YES, BUT...

The Big Breakfast
What are the words teenagers use most? I reckon 'Yes, but…' must be in there near the top of the list. A strange thing happens once we get past the age of eight or nine. Adults just don't seem to understand how unfair or plain stupid their expectations are. 'Yes, but…' was used a lot in my house as we grew up.

Jesus has a 'Yes, but…' being thrown at him here. 'Love God with all your heart. Let me help you. Come on, it's what you were made for. And when you love me, you'll grow to love your neighbour too.' This is what Jesus has been trying to tell the young man. He just can't get it, though. Instead he says to Jesus, 'Yes, but who is my neighbour?' Jesus must have been heartbroken. The young man hadn't heard what Jesus was saying to him. 'Who is my neighbour?' was just another trick question, and both Jesus and the young man knew it.

Continental
It isn't a good idea to set out to trick someone intentionally. It often makes a fool of them, which isn't the Jesus way of living with other people.

Coffee
Lord Jesus, forgive me for the times when I say 'Yes, but…' to you. Whenever I think I know best, there's always more I can learn from you.

Orange Juice

But he wanted to justify himself, so he asked Jesus, 'And who is my neighbour?'

LUKE 10:29 NIV

THAT OLD DEVIL CALLED PRIDE

The Big Breakfast

Let's take one last look at the motives of the 'expert in the law'. He and his other religious friends had distorted God's law into a contemporary version of religious respectability. It was a harsh, legalistic and oppressive application of the teaching from the Old Testament. Why? Why in the world had something that was good become so distorted, so that guidelines for living which were designed for all that was good and right in human life had been reduced to a code of behaviour that would merely be a measure of human acceptability.

Could it be that old devil called pride? To follow a list of rules means that I'm in charge. To follow Jesus means that Jesus is in charge. Pride deceives us into believing that the inner life of the heart can be transformed and changed by outward activity. As we watch our TVs and see day after day the litany of evil things that human beings do to one another, have we ever stopped to ask what the real source of that evil is?

Continental

Jesus' one concern in all the exchanges he had with people was to make them see the reality of what was in their hearts.

Coffee

Lord Jesus, show me what is in my heart. I live every day as if it's okay. Please give me the gift of a kingdom heart.

Orange Juice

In reply Jesus said: 'A man was going down from Jerusalem to Jericho, when he fell into the hands of robbers. They stripped him of his clothes, beat him and went away, leaving him half-dead.'

LUKE 10:30 NIV

THE INVISIBLE MAN

The Big Breakfast

In a TV documentary which followed the lives of four homeless men, I was struck by a comment made by one of them. When he was asked what the worst thing was about being homeless, he replied, 'Being invisible.' You can just picture it: the sleeping bag in a doorway in the middle of the day. What happens? We all walk past. He's invisible.

Jesus decides to answer the question, 'Who is my neighbour?' by telling a story. His stories were full of pictures of everyday things and places. The road from Jerusalem to Jericho was no exception. It was notorious for its danger. People travelling it knew they could be robbed. There's another important picture in this story too. The man who has been robbed has also been beaten, left unconscious and stripped of his clothes, which means he can't be identified. He can't speak for himself, and because he has no clothes it's impossible to tell where he's from.

Do we need to know a person's background before we help them?

Continental

Who are the invisible people around us today? Who are the people we never get close to? We can't help someone who is hurting unless we get close.

Coffee

Lord, forgive me for allowing people to stay invisible. I'm determined to change that, but I need your help.

Orange Juice

It happened that a Jewish priest was going down that road. When he saw the man, he walked by on the other side.

LUKE 10:31 NCV

RULE-BOOK RELIGION

The Big Breakfast

When you go to see a play, it makes sense to buy a programme before it starts. For one thing, it will give you some background to the characters and will explain what their relationship is to one another.

Knowing a bit of background about the characters in this well-known drama of the 'Good Samaritan' will help us to get the point of the story Jesus told. Player No. 1, then, is the priest. The priest was a man whose livelihood depended on him keeping the religious rules, especially the rules for priests. He wasn't allowed to touch a dead man. In fact, he wasn't even allowed to get close to a dead man. He was also only supposed to help certain people, so he had to be able to identify who people were before he could get involved. On top of that, he was a leader, so he was concerned about what people thought of him. Life for him was a list of do's and don'ts.

Continental

The priest was a victim of the religious rule book. For him, the way to please God was to keep the rules. Jesus didn't think so.

Coffee

We judge the priest very harshly, don't we? How could he put rules before people in need? Stop and think. Have you ever done that?

Orange Juice

Next, a Levite came there, and after he went over and looked at the man, he walked by on the other side of the road.

LUKE 10:32 NCV

The Big Breakfast

An American psychologist, fascinated by the story of the Good Samaritan, once did a research project among theological students at Princeton College in New Jersey. He asked four students, known to be popular among their peers and of general good nature, to prepare a sermon on the Good Samaritan. They each had to give their sermon at a set place and time. The psychologist then arranged for four other students to pretend to be ill or injured at some point close to the venue where the sermons were to be given. Every one of the theological students rushed past the sick student without stopping. They all said they had an important sermon to give and hadn't time to help. Even the psychologist was shocked.

In the story Jesus told, the Levite, another religious man, also passed by the beaten man. Was he too busy? Perhaps he thought he was. It's also possible that he was a copycat. The priest hadn't stopped, so why should he? The Jericho road was very straight, and the Levite would have seen the priest. He knew he hadn't stopped.

Continental

There are always good reasons for not doing the right thing. At least we can convince ourselves in this way. The question is, what would Jesus have done?

Coffee

Lord Jesus, help me to be influenced and guided by your values and standards in everything I do.

Orange Juice

Then a Samaritan travelling down the road came to where the hurt man was. When he saw the man, he felt very sorry for him.

LUKE 10:33 NCV

WE ALL BLEED RED BLOOD

The Big Breakfast

This drama is getting more interesting by the moment. What's Jesus saying now? A Samaritan stopped to help? They were enemies, the Samaritans and Jews, forever at one another's throats. For the hero of Jesus' story to be a Samaritan is astonishing. The people listening to his words would certainly have been taken aback, at the very least.

I want you to imagine a Northern Irish Protestant stopping in a Catholic area of Belfast to help someone; or a white South African in a black township; or a Kosovo-Albanian in Serb territory. Can you visualize this? That's the kind of picture Jesus paints through this story.

Why is it that we can so easily imagine our friends, our family, the people amongst whom we live, being Good Samaritans, while we believe our 'enemies' to be less than human? The same compassion, sympathy, goodness and love that flows through our veins is also found in those we hate.

Continental

The award-winning journalist Fergal Keene has reported from many countries where racial and ethnic differences have torn communities apart. Of Northern Ireland he once said, 'Tears and heartbreak are the same whether you are Catholic or Protestant.'

Coffee

Lord Jesus, I hate to admit that my heart has prejudice and hate in it, but it does. Please forgive me. Help me to change.

Orange Juice
The Samaritan went to him, poured olive oil and wine on his wounds and bandaged them.

LUKE 10:34A NCV

HIDDEN MEANINGS

The Big Breakfast
I'm going to Kenya this summer with 10 young people. None of us has been there before, so we decided that a fun way to find out a little about Africa was to spend an evening watching the movie *Out of Africa*. Now, I love this movie. I've watched it two or three times, so I was blown away when I realized I'd missed one of the main twists of the plot. How could I not have seen it before?

The thing was, it was slipped in very subtly. It was just one brief scene that had to be put together with another much later on in the movie.

There are a few subtle twists in this story of Jesus too. Oil and wine were often used to clean wounds. They were also used in worship services as symbols of God's love. In the Old Testament God is seen putting a bandage on the wounds of his people. The twist that Jesus put into his plot would have been a big shock to the people listening to him. God is represented in his story by a Samaritan, a person who was hated.

Continental
God will surprise us all the time. He loves and reaches out to those we hate in the same way that he reaches out to us.

Coffee
The values of the kingdom will always be shocking to us. It's what we do with them that matters to God.

Orange Juice
Then he put the hurt man on his own donkey and took him to an inn where he cared for him.

LUKE 10:34B NCV

WALKING BESIDE THE DONKEY

The Big Breakfast
Some stories have so many twists to them that it's hard to keep up. The Samaritan put the wounded man on his donkey in order to take him to safety. That was the obvious thing to do, considering that they were in a dangerous place, with robbers hiding in the hills above them. What is not so obvious to us, reading the story all these years later, is that the Samaritan's actions were another real shock to the people listening to the story being told by Jesus. By putting the man on his donkey, the Samaritan was giving up his place to a stranger. By doing this, he changed from being a wealthy merchant (most likely to have been his profession) to being a servant. In Middle Eastern culture, the only person to walk beside an animal while another person was riding on it was a servant or slave. Even today, it would be pretty difficult to get a travel guide to ride with you. They insist on leading the donkey. It's all about respect.

Continental
Throughout the Bible we find many pictures like this one, showing people who give up their rights or position to serve others. Most significant of these is Jesus himself.

Coffee
Lord Jesus, it's pretty clear that one of the big things about being a Christian is putting other people first. I'm not very good at that. Please help me.

Orange Juice

The next day, the Samaritan brought out two silver coins, gave them to the innkeeper, and said, 'Take care of this man. If you spend more money on him, I will pay it back to you when I come again.'

LUKE 10:35 NCV

BILL ME LATER

The Big Breakfast

Now, why would the Samaritan do this? He'd never met this man before. He didn't know who he was, or where he was from. He might even have been an enemy. In fact, he probably was from a community that hated Samaritans. It was one thing to get him out of the danger zone, but something else altogether to pay for his care. Who does that sort of thing?

God does. God does that sort of thing. A friend of mine was a minister in the United States for a few years. He told me about meeting a lady in a park one day. She wasn't from the same church tradition as him, but she did want to talk to a priest, she said. Her church had thrown her out because they didn't understand her lifestyle. She hated them, and God. She reckoned they had both let her down. As she talked to my friend, however, she felt understood. She felt release and healing. She turned to my friend and said, 'When I couldn't find God, he found me. Thank you.'

Continental

God's investment in us is a love gift. He comes and finds us to give us this gift, at no cost to us, but at enormous cost to him.

Coffee

Our salvation is free, but to follow Jesus will cost us everything we have.

Orange Juice
The next day, the Samaritan brought out two silver coins, gave them to the innkeeper, and said, 'Take care of this man…'

LUKE 10:35A NCV

THE W.W.J.D. CHALLENGE

The Big Breakfast
The TV show *The Simpsons* is well established as one of those great institutions of our times. Here is a great Homer quote: 'Careful now, these are dangerous streets for us upper-lower-middle-class types. So avoid eye contact, watch your pockets and suspect everyone.' Great, isn't it? Classic Homer talk.

I don't know whether the Samaritan was an upper-lower-middle-class type, but he was certainly walking into a dangerous street when he led his donkey into Jericho with this beaten, half-dead man on it. Being from 'another tribe', there was a pretty good chance that he'd be blamed for the man's injuries. There wouldn't be time for explanations. Assumptions would be made simply because of who he was. Yet he took the man to an inn and stayed the night with him. For the sake of the other person, he accepted the possibility of being wrongly accused.

If you knew that you ran the risk of being beaten up, or possibly even murdered, would you have hung around?

Continental
To follow Jesus could mean that looking out for our own safety is our second priority in some circumstances. Are you prepared for that?

Coffee
Do you know about the W.W.J.D. challenge? What Would Jesus Do? Think carefully about what it might mean to 'do what Jesus would do' in every situation.

Orange Juice

Then Jesus said, 'Which one of these three men do you think was a neighbour to the man who was attacked by the robbers?'

LUKE 10:36 NCV

SO THAT'S WHAT IT MEANS

The Big Breakfast

I was in a hurry to get to a doctor's appointment one day. I needed a parking space, and I needed it now. It was lunchtime. I only had an hour free. I spied a free space, the only one in the street, so I nipped quickly into it. There was a man waving at me in an irritated way, but I just ignored him. I had no time for any petty nonsense that day. I later regretted that thought. The man was trying to tell me that I'd driven up a one-way street and that the police had nicked a guy a few minutes earlier for doing the same thing.

I really appreciated this man for being bothered to tell me my mistake. He could have ignored me and walked past on the other side. Is Jesus telling us through this story to be good to other people? To look out for them, and always try to help? Well, yes, but it goes a lot deeper than that! Living a good life is not the same as living a kingdom life.

Continental

The Good Samaritan story is loaded with messages. It's an attack on racial prejudice and religious bigotry. It's also a challenge to help anyone in need, and to put other people first. It's strong stuff.

Coffee

Lord Jesus, I'm slowly realizing that being a Christian is not about trying to live a good life. It's about letting you transform every attitude I have. Please do it.

Orange Juice

Then Jesus said, 'Which one … was a neighbour…?' The expert on the law answered, 'The one who showed him mercy.'

LUKE 10:36-37 NCV

SHE SAID 'YES'

The Big Breakfast

When she was asked by one of her classmates if she believed in God, Cassie Bernall said 'Yes'. So he shot her. We all know the story of Columbine High School in Littleton, Colorado. Thirteen young people were murdered there when two of their classmates rampaged through the school on 20 April 1999. It has been said that the two boys were cheering and laughing, saying things like, 'We've been waiting to do this our whole lives!' Why? Why did Eric and Dylan do this terrible thing?

We're still shocked by the Columbine killings. It was just an ordinary neighbourhood. Why there? Why Littleton? All kinds of explanations have been given. One that struck me particularly was that Eric and Dylan had been left out of things by their peer group. They had been laughed at for being different. They felt rejected and unloved. Why did they do it? No one will ever really know. Could it be that a perceived lack of mercy and love from their classmates drove them to these appalling actions?

Continental

Mercy: the action of loving and caring because of what is in your heart, not because the other person deserves it.

Coffee

Lord Jesus, it seems to me that mercy is what your heart towards us is all about. Thank you, and please give me the same heart towards other people.

Orange Juice

The expert on the law answered, 'The one who showed him mercy.' Jesus said to him, 'Then go and do what he did.'

LUKE 10:37 NCV

SPIRITUAL REVIEW

The Big Breakfast

How are you doing on the self-examination front? We all have to do this kind of thing these days. Performance indicators are the big thing. Are you meeting your targets or personal goals at work, with this assignment or that project? Even in the gym we have to set ourselves personal achievement targets.

What about a spiritual review? Have you checked out how you're doing on that score recently? Are there any personal bests to brag about?

This 'expert in the law' who had been debating with Jesus found himself becoming the subject of a personal appraisal. He had begun the debate. It seemed as if he was trying to point out to Jesus how well he knew his Bible. He reckoned he had it together. Jesus, however, skilfully showed him how much more there is to following God than sticking to rules. I like Jesus' style. He gets the man to see his mistakes without rubbishing him as a person.

Continental

God is always gracious to us. He knows we get things wrong all the time. Helping us to put it right is his business, but he will wait for us to ask.

Coffee

Do that personal spiritual inventory today. Get God to help you. He'll give you good targets and all the help in the world to meet them.

Orange Juice

O L ORD, you have searched me and know me. You know when I sit and when I rise; you perceive my thoughts from afar.

PSALM 139:1-2 NIV

INSIDE OUT

The Big Breakfast

We used to laugh at Mum. When she wanted to get hold of one of us, because there were six for her to choose from, she would often go through all our names before she got to the person she really wanted. She would then tut at herself in frustration. Poor lady. She always had far too many things on her mind. To get the right name straight off was a struggle.

God knows our name, and he gets it right every time. That's a good feeling, isn't it? He also sees what we get up to. Scary as that may be, it's actually very, very good news. Nothing can shock him. He's beyond that. Nothing can put him off. There's also plenty that excites him. We have so much potential! All he wants is to get into partnership with us.

Continental

Matthew 10:30 reminds us that even the hairs on our heads are counted. Now that is amazing.

Coffee

How do you feel about yourself today? Do you feel special? You are, and that's a fact. You are known and accepted inside out. You belong.

Orange Juice

You are all around me – in front and at the back – and have put your hand on me. Your knowledge is amazing to me; it is more than I can understand.

PSALM 139:5-6 NCV

GOD IS FOR YOU

The Big Breakfast

When God makes a decision to be involved with you it isn't half-hearted. He is totally for you. Totally. Listen to what he says in Jeremiah 32:40: 'I will never stop doing good to them.' Now those are the words of a God who is for you.

David, who wrote this Psalm, understood that God was all around him, looking out for him. In fact, he couldn't get away from God and that was the most excellent thing in his life. He knew that God was totally for him. Being surrounded by God meant he felt very safe.

Continental

'If God is for us, who can be against us?' (Romans 8:32) How does that grab you? The creator of the universe is looking out for you!

Coffee

Lord, I so often allow the problem points in my life to stop me seeing how close you are, how much you care and how much you want to help. Forgive me.

Orange Juice
…even there your hand will guide me, your right hand will hold me fast.

PSALM 139:10 NIV

SIGNPOSTS

The Big Breakfast
How do we know God is always guiding us? Isn't it all down to a bit of luck, good or bad?

Maybe Joseph in the Old Testament can help. He had jealous brothers, and a stupid father who was no doubt responsible for causing the brothers to be jealous. Joseph himself had an arrogant side. He boasted a lot. He was also a silly dreamer. He saw things in his dreams that he would have kept to himself if he'd had any wit at all. But no, Big Mouth tells his brothers that they will one day bow down to him as a king. Imagine it. They weren't happy. So Joseph was sold as a slave. His brothers reckoned that was the last of him.

Years later, however, Joseph turned up again, and guess what? The brothers bowed down to him because of his powerful position. Read all about it in Genesis chapters 37 to 46. It's an amazing story. The main thing to notice is that God was there all along. He was in charge of things; he was watching out for Joseph and guiding what happened.

Continental
The signposts along the way include circumstances that come together in an unexpected way; a helpful word from a friend; a disappointment that later you can see was a good thing.

Coffee
The fact that God is guiding us doesn't mean that we stop thinking for ourselves. He works with us to guide us by or through the decisions we make.

Orange Juice

For you created my inmost being; you knit me together in my mother's womb.

PSALM 139:13 NIV

IT'S A MIRACLE EVERY TIME

The Big Breakfast

My sister had a beautiful baby girl recently. She was three weeks early. I've never seen or held a little girl so small, so tiny, so perfect. Minute little fingernails, perfectly formed; beautiful eyelashes; gurgles; funny little contortions of her face that for now are a smile. Just four pounds, eight ounces of weight – and yet packed inside are the heart, lungs, kidneys, liver, blood vessels, muscles and ligaments that keep her alive. And a tiny brain, that vital organ that tells her to cry when she's hungry, to suck at her mother's breast, to sleep and wake, to react to light and heat and cold. When I saw her she was only six hours old.

It's a miracle. Every time it happens it's a miracle. A tiny egg that the naked eye can't see is fertilized. It grows gently and slowly, and inside it bones and flesh are joined together. A wonderful little person is formed who one day will breathe and think, laugh and cry, dance and sing. It's an absolute miracle.

Continental

The gift of life is a gift from God every time. No matter how you feel about yourself today, you're an amazing creation that was specially planned.

Coffee

A life that involves this degree of intricate creativity and engineering should never be flushed down a hospital waste chute like some piece of useless garbage.

Orange Juice
I praise you because you made me in an amazing and wonderful way.

PSALM 139:14 NCV

ORBITER 3

The Big Breakfast
On 21 March 1999 Orbiter 3 was spotted over the desert in southern Egypt. The hot-air balloon came into land after 20 days. Brian and Bertrand had done it. They were the first to make it round the world in a hot-air balloon. What an achievement! There had been scary moments, for sure. When they were flying 40,000 feet above the Pacific Ocean, with nothing but sea for miles, Bertrand began to pass out. Brian wasn't feeling too good either. 'A switch kind of flicked in my head,' said Brian. 'We're being poisoned.' They were. It was carbon monoxide.

Brian Jones and his co-pilot took on a tough challenge. They pushed themselves to the edge again and again, but discovered the kind of stuff we humans are made of: not just physical strength, but mental, emotional and spiritual strength too.

God did an amazing job when he came up with the human design. David, the man writing this Psalm, is blown away by it. It's so great that he can't get his head round it.

Continental
Take time to think about 'you' today. Write down three good things about yourself that contribute to your uniqueness. Now thank God for how he made you.

Coffee
Lord Jesus, thank you for the care that went into the making of me. Help me to see the possibilities that exist within me.

Orange Juice
God, examine me and know my heart… See if there is any bad thing in me.
Lead me on the road to everlasting life.

PSALM 139:23-24 NCV

CHOICES

The Big Breakfast
I think David is feeling a wee bit ashamed here.
He's been getting very excited about the good
job God did when he created us humans. In fact,
you almost feel David will go into orbit because he's so
excited and overcome by the wonderful way God made us.
He's come down to earth now, though. 'Take a look at my
heart, God,' he says. 'It's not so wonderful in there any more.'

I guess David realized something very important. When
God first made things, including us, it was all perfect.
Everything worked together well. But God took some risks at
that time. He wanted people who would make choices, who
would respond to his love and the love of other people. We
make choices, good ones and bad ones. The amazing thing
about God, of course, is that he wants to help sort out the
consequences of our bad choices. Like David in this Psalm,
we need to come to God and ask him for some help.

Continental
When we become
Christians we begin a
journey with God
that allows him to
restore us to the way
we were meant to
be in the first place.

Coffee
When you think about yourself, do you reckon you need God's help to make
the best of your potential, or will your own efforts do?

Orange Juice
Someone in the crowd said to Jesus, 'Teacher, tell my brother to divide with me the property our father left us.'

LUKE 12:13 NCV

YOUR NO. 1 JOB

The Big Breakfast
There's a storm brewing, a big family bust-up. Two brothers can't agree over their legacy, and they want Jesus to sort it out. Well, one of them wants Jesus to sort it out. It makes you wonder what happened before this guy got so desperate that he had to shout out at Jesus in public. Had he tried to work things out with his brother and just not managed it? Had he felt let down by his brother's attitude? Or had he just assumed that his brother would try to cheat him out of what was his by right?

Whatever the deal, one thing is clear: he wants his share. He's fighting for his rights. It must have been a big shock to him, to find that Jesus wasn't interested. 'Who said I should judge or decide between you?' Jesus wasn't interested in rights of this kind. Jesus had given up all the amazing rights and privileges that were his, and had come to earth to serve people. He was hardly going to take sides in such a situation.

Continental
How do you think of Jesus? Is he Mr Fix-it for you, or a big Santa Claus who always gives us what we want? Take a closer look.

Coffee
To follow Jesus means becoming like Jesus. That means living like Jesus, which means that serving God and other people is your No. 1 job.

Orange Juice

Then Jesus said to them, 'Be careful and guard against all kinds of greed. Life is not measured by how much one owns.'

LUKE 12:15 NCV

WHO WANTS TO BE A MILLIONAIRE?

The Big Breakfast

The pressure is huge. Should he take what he's got and run, or risk it all, go for the next question and become a millionaire? Chris Tarrant can't help him. He must get the question absolutely right first time. What a lonely moment. What does it matter, though? It's just another game show. It'll be somebody else tomorrow.

Game shows, the National Lottery, scratch cards — they're in your face every day. What has this done to us? I reckon it has probably turned us into fun-loving but rather misguided people. The message of the game show and the lottery is that money makes you happy. The more you have, the better things will be for you. So go on, take the risk, go for the next question, get the million.

Jesus must be so sad as he watches all this. He knows that the more we have, the more we want. 'Be careful,' he says, 'guard against all kinds of greed.' Your life shouldn't be measured by, or depend on, what you own. The trouble is, we're continually being told just the opposite.

Continental

Jesus would be happier with what Tony Campolo once said: 'The prize is not what you get, it is what you become.'

Coffee

Ask Jesus to help you see the things in your life that subtly draw you to the 'must have' mindset. Then determine to live the kingdom life.

Orange Juice

Then Jesus told this story: 'There was a rich man who had some land, which grew a good crop. He thought to himself, "What will I do? I have no place to keep all my crops… I will tear down my barns and build bigger ones."'

LUKE 12:16-18 NCV

HOW ARE YOU USING IT?

The Big Breakfast

She's worth somewhere in the region of £22 million and she's only 25 years old. Mel B, Scary Spice, has done okay, don't you think? She's one of the most successful pop stars around today. Talking recently about having money, she said a few things worth noting. For example, she doesn't think of herself as rich, but as someone who can help her family and friends.

Jesus has just warned the people listening to him about becoming greedy. Don't make the mistake of measuring your life by wealth, he says. He goes on to tell a story about a wealthy farmer. This is obviously an important point he's making. His story is repeating the warning he has just made. He's painting a picture of how some people behave. When they have it good and make more money than they need, they just spend it on themselves or save it for themselves. Building a bigger barn isn't a good idea. It's not God's idea. Wealth comes to us as a gift and we must use it wisely.

Continental

You may not think you're rich. Nonetheless, whatever you have is a gift from God. How are you using it?

Coffee

Lord Jesus, it's so easy to think of what I have as only for my own use and pleasure. I'm sorry.

Orange Juice

'I have enough good things stored to last for many years. Rest, eat, drink and enjoy life!' But God said to him, 'Foolish man! Tonight your life will be taken from you…'

LUKE 12:19-20 NCV

EAT, DRINK AND BE MERRY – NOT

The Big Breakfast

There's a lot of it around these days. 'Have a good time. Enjoy yourself. Go on, why not? There isn't much else to get excited about!' Despite the fact that our times are so technologically advanced, nobody seems to be very hopeful about the future. In fact, 'future' is a scary word. It's best not to think about it. Live it up now.

The good news is that the future doesn't need to be scary. Walking with Jesus and getting onto his wavelength puts a whole new colour on things. He has a much better deal on offer. There are a few guidelines that are important, though.

He warns us not to get tempted to go down the 'eat, drink and be merry' route. Our lives should be more than that – God expects more of us. Don't think you can do what you like and it won't matter. If you're following Jesus, it does matter. It matters a great deal.

Continental

The rich man in the story made one big mistake: he left God out of the picture. He thought he was in charge. Not so.

Coffee

Lord Jesus, all I have is a gift from you. Help me to think more about the surplus you allow me to have, and then use it properly.

Orange Juice
But God said to him, 'Foolish man! Tonight your life will be taken from you. So who will get those things you have prepared for yourself?'

LUKE 12:20 NCV

THE BARN MAN

The Big Breakfast
God's thundering response must have been a huge shock. This man was going to die. It really wasn't important that he had barns full of good stuff.

I don't know about you, but I've read this story many times and I always think the barn man was a total fool. He was selfish too, really selfish. It's strange, however, that I never seem to see *myself* as being the barn man. I can somehow read the story and get all judgemental about the rich man – but the thing is, if I'm open to Jesus, if I'm listening to the point he's making, I should see that he's got *me* in mind! My barns are very full too. Jesus says, 'You fool.'

Is Jesus making a virtue out of poverty? Should we only keep enough to buy the essentials and give the rest of our money away? I don't imagine that's quite the point Jesus has in mind. It's much more likely that he's emphasizing the importance of the attitudes in our hearts, which will determine how we behave towards God and others.

Continental
There are two investments this foolish man could have made. Firstly, he could have given time to family and friends. Secondly, he could have trusted God, not himself, and lived out of that trust rather than following selfish ambition.

Coffee
Lord Jesus, it's so easy to be blind to my own selfishness. Help me to see what's really going on with me. Help me to change.

Orange Juice

This is how it will be with anyone who stores up things for himself but is not rich towards God.

LUKE 12:21 NIV

YOU CAN TAKE IT WITH YOU!

The Big Breakfast

In other words, life is a gift. Any surplus wealth we get is a gift also, because God does give surplus as a gift. Both are on loan, however. The person who thinks that security and a good life are found in material wealth is a fool. Life is good when we invest in it by 'giving to God'.

How do we give to God? How do we become 'rich towards him'? He has all he needs. Why would he want anything from us? And isn't this a contradiction of what we hear from Jesus elsewhere? You can't earn eternal life – it's God's freely given, undeserved gift.

There's no contradiction. There never is, even if it seems that way. We just need to understand it properly. What God wants back from us is the willing gift of our lives to him. Why? So that he can control us and remove all our freedom? No. So that he can give us the life for which we were created. On our own, we usually mess it up.

Continental

Giving our lives back to God isn't just about us. It's about pleasing God because he's worth it.

Coffee

There's only one type of wealth you can take with you when you die, and that's the investment you've made in your relationship with God.

Orange Juice
He remembers his covenant for ever, the word he commanded, for a thousand generations.

PSALM 105:8 NIV

THE HAT

The Big Breakfast
When I was 16, I was a rock star, travelling the country with my guitar slung around my neck, performing at this gig and that. My mates were really jealous – all those famous people, being famous myself. When the recording deal fell through, I woke up. I was only a rock star in my dreams.

I actually was a singer. I even made a recording, and I did make it onto a few stages. On one memorable occasion I was singing at a religious meeting. A friend of mine had asked me to come as he was preaching. At the end a man in a grey suit thanked us. His words about me went something like this: 'Our wee friend was good, but we wish she'd worn a hat.' It beats me what wearing a hat had to do with being a rock star!

It's funny how I remember that remark. Our memories can make us laugh. They can make us cry, too. We may even block them out. God has a great memory. He remembers the promises he has made to us, and he keeps them.

Continental
Good memories are a blessing. Bad memories are a curse. They can leave us wishing we were dead. God remembers his promises. He has promised us the best, which includes the healing of memories.

Coffee
Are you hurting today because of a bad memory? God is a wonderful Father with a long memory, and he's waiting for the opportunity to heal that hurt.

Orange Juice

Isaac brought her into the tent of his mother Sarah, and he married Rebekah. So she became his wife, and he loved her.

GENESIS 24:67 NIV

READ ALL ABOUT IT

The Big Breakfast

Ally McBeal – now there's a girl who's unlucky in love; or just plain stupid. I wish she would forget Billy. He's a monster on her shoulder. Mind you, we all got very interested when he eventually kissed her. There are a lot of people on that show who are a bit messed up by past relationships.

Isaac and Rebekah – this is a wonderful love story. Read all about it in Genesis 24. The Bible has a whole collection of great love stories. The story of Ruth and Boaz is another one. They had a different way of finding their mates in Bible times. I'm not sure how well I would have coped if my Dad had made all the decisions for me! On the other hand, when I look at the mess a lot of us get ourselves into, maybe it wouldn't be so bad.

We make a lot of mistakes in love, and yet we all want to be loved, to have that special relationship. God wants to help us in this part of our lives too.

Continental

It's sad to see that these days advice on how to find a boyfriend or girlfriend all seems to come from horoscopes in popular magazines. I'd give that advice a big miss.

Coffee

God is very interested in all of your life. *All* of it. Give him a chance to help you in this important area. He wants to help you avoid messing up.

Orange Juice
Create in me a pure heart, O God, and renew a steadfast spirit within me.

PSALM 51:10 NIV

RULES ARE GOOD

The Big Breakfast
Christina Aguilera and Britney Spears are battling it out. Who really is the 'Teen Queen of Pop'?
For the two girls who started out as friends in the show *The Mickey Mouse Club* (1992), the question now being asked is which of them is the 'real babe'. So we must judge them on their bodies, their best physical assets and, yes, whether or not they're virgins.

We live in a sex-saturated society. We can't get through a single day without somebody somewhere telling us how great sex is. God has a lot to say about sex. He thinks it's great – after all, he invented it. But he has given us a few guidelines, 'directions for use' if you like. When we ignore these, we get into a lot of bother. King David discovered this. He took another man's wife to bed with him. He may have enjoyed it, but it eventually drove him to murder her husband in order to cover up what he'd done wrong.

In this Psalm he's asking God to give him a pure heart. He realizes that things got out of hand because his heart and his desires were all screwed up.

Continental
A few years ago, the Baptist Church in America began a campaign called 'Proud to be Pure'. Teenagers signed a pledge not to have sex until they got married. *More* magazine wrote it off as nonsense. What do you think?

Coffee
God knows that our sexual drive is a strong one that can take us over. He wants to help us control it. Ask him to help you.

Orange Juice

The LORD is close to the broken-hearted and saves those who are crushed in spirit.

PSALM 34:18 NIV

BROKEN PIECES

The Big Breakfast

There must be a million love songs about broken hearts. I'm sure you can easily think of one.

Maybe you'd rather not because right now your own heart hurts too much. Or perhaps you have a vivid memory of a time when it did. It's pretty much impossible to get through all that relationship stuff without taking an arrow in the heart.

God is great at rebuilding relationships. His whole purpose with us is restoring that which is broken between him and us – which we broke in the first place. I reckon God knows all about a broken heart.

There's a great line in the film *City of Angels*: 'He gave those bozos down there the greatest gift in the universe – free will.' So he did. That freedom can allow us to be very selfish, especially when it comes to relationships. We forget that another person is involved. We get caught up with ourselves and what we want.

If your heart is broken, God knows what that's like. He's very close to you, even if it doesn't feel like it.

Continental

I remember well the first real broken heart I had. I cried and cried, and felt I would die from the pain. One of my close friends hugged me for a long time.

Coffee

If your heart is breaking and you think you'll suffocate from the pain, just know that God's great arms are hugging you very tightly.

Orange Juice

'I say this because I know what I am planning for you,' says the LORD. 'I have good plans for you, not plans to hurt you. I will give you hope and a good future.'

JEREMIAH 29:11 NCV

A MAN CALLED DAVID

The Big Breakfast

My friend David told me a marvellous story recently. He'd been for a job interview the day before. When he got home, his eight-year-old son overheard him telling his wife how he'd got on. Jonathan came running into the kitchen and said, 'Daddy, does God have plans? Did God plan that the man who was interviewing you for that job would know that a man called David would come for the interview, and would he know that God wants a man called David to get that job?' What about that for insight from an eight-year-old?

Does God have plans? He certainly does. He has terrific plans – big plans about the future of this planet and the people living on it; plans for whole nations of people, from every ethnic and cultural background; plans that the sun will keep shining and the rain will keep falling so all those people can grow food to feed themselves. The biggest deal of all is that he has plans for us as individuals, plans that are good, very good indeed.

Continental

You might ask, 'What about all those times when the rain didn't come, or came too much and too often? What about the innocent victims of war or famine? Were those part of God's plan?'

Coffee

God's plans are always good, but we need to work in partnership with him, not against him. We need to follow the way he tells us to live, not ignore him.

Orange Juice
We have around us many people whose lives tell us what faith means.

HEBREWS 12:1A NCV

STORY TIME

The Big Breakfast
One of the things we do well in Ireland, where I live, is tell stories about one another. When they're told with a bit of Irish 'blarney' thrown in, they can sound like bestsellers! The great thing about these stories is that you get to hear about people's lives – the fun stuff, the rough stuff, the good and bad stuff.

I reckon that God wants us to get into telling stories. That way we get to hear the great things other Christians have done and how they've handled their lives. This verse in Hebrews is trying to tell us how much we need one another. 'Being a Christian' isn't supposed to be worked out all by ourselves. If we look at other followers of Jesus, we will learn from them. In fact, by looking at their lives, we will get some help in understanding about faith, and that's a tough one to understand sometimes.

Continental
There are a whole load of famous people who would fit the bill here – Mother Teresa, Martin Luther King Jr… Think today of someone you know personally, whose life helps you to understand faith better.

Coffee
Lord Jesus, thank you for the people who have lived great, faithful lives. Help me to learn from them.

Orange Juice

Let us look only to Jesus, the One who began our faith and who makes it perfect.

HEBREWS 12:2A NCV

The Big Breakfast

When I was a kid I used to go to my Gran's for part of the summer holidays. She always bought Rice Krispies for breakfast. The back of the cereal box always had a puzzle or game on it. We needed something to do on those rainy days! I remember once the back of the box had the boys from Liverpool on it – Paul, John, George and Ringo. (Yes, it was a long time ago!) They were everywhere in those days.

We still live in a celebrity-obsessed culture. How many of those gossip magazines are out there now, telling us who has just married whom, or who has split up from whom, and all the other stuff that's going on in their lives? We're fascinated by it. We're also addicted to it. We want to know all about these people. Do we secretly think they have inside knowledge on how to sort things out? Whether we like it or not, we look up to our celebs. They're our mentors.

Continental

Celebrities are human too. They'll get some things right and others wrong, just like us. If you want to look up to someone, look up to Jesus.

Coffee

Jesus is much more than a great mentor. He's right in there with us, working things out so that our lives and our faith grow.

Orange Juice
By helping each other with your troubles, you truly obey the law of Christ.

GALATIANS 6:2 NCV

A LITTLE HELP FROM MY FRIENDS

The Big Breakfast
'A Little Help From My Friends' is a great song. The Beatles had loads of them. Even after all these years, we're still singing the lines.

One of the best things about being part of the Christian family is all those good friends we can make, people who are there for us. Part of their job as Christians is to be there for us, just as it's part of our job to be there for them.

To be a Christian is to belong to an amazing club that has members all over the world. And there's more: everyone in that club is there for you. They're there to help when you're in trouble. But you need to let them know when you're in trouble. There was a really sad story in our local news recently. A young girl killed herself because she couldn't take the bullying at school any more. Nobody actually knew she was being bullied until it was too late. Why didn't she tell someone?

Continental
We keep things to ourselves because we're afraid or ashamed, or because we reckon we can work it out for ourselves. Sharing is better.

Coffee
Talking about some of the really deep things that concern you takes courage and trust. Give a Christian friend the benefit of the doubt and tell them what's bothering you.

Orange Juice
Jesus said to them, 'When you pray, say: "Father, may your name always be kept holy." '

LUKE 11:2A NCV

IT'S HOW YOU DO IT

The Big Breakfast
What's the word you hear used most often? It's probably God's name. I often wonder why things turned out like that. Why don't we hear people say, 'Oh my Buddha!' or 'For Mother Nature's sake!' It's strange that we laugh at that idea. I don't know why God's name has become an easy swearword, but I do know that God doesn't like it. In fact, it upsets him a great deal.

The big question is, why don't we Christians do something about it? We listen to the misuse of God's name every day, but we rarely challenge it. I know: it would seem prudish, or far too religious, or perhaps an invasion into other people's rights and space. I guess it's how we do things that's important. I agree that we have no right to tell other people how to speak or what language they can use. We do have a right, however, to defend the reputation and dignity of our Lord. This is a political correctness well worth fighting for.

Continental
There is much about God, and about being a Christian, that's treated as irrelevant today. There's nothing irrelevant about God, and the way we use his name does matter.

Coffee
Lord Jesus, I have to say that I've become far too familiar with the misuse of your name. Help me to defend your reputation in wise ways.

Orange Juice
Jesus said to them, 'When you pray, say: "…May your kingdom come." '

LUKE 11:2 NCV

WHEN THE RESOLUTION COMES

The Big Breakfast
When I walk down the High Street on a Saturday afternoon, I often come across one of those 'street preachers' – a wee man with a microphone in one hand and a big black book in the other. Sometimes he'll have a placard saying, 'Repent, for the kingdom of God is at hand!' He's trying to let people know that they need Jesus in their lives.

The words on his placard interest me: 'The kingdom of God is at hand.' What does that mean? It makes me think of these words in the prayer Jesus taught us. We're to pray that God's kingdom will come. Is God planning a coup? Are we to be the army that makes it happen?

It seems to me that what Jesus wants us to pray for isn't some mad revolution that will take people by force. Rather, he wants us to pray that they will change their allegiance because they want to. It will be a revolution in their hearts, and it will change things for ever.

Continental
We are Jesus' followers, and he is asking us to pray that this heart revolution will happen for other people. Think about it: our best weapon in the fight for lives is prayer.

Coffee
Lord Jesus, if I'm honest, I usually pray for my own concerns. It's a bit like bringing you my shopping list. Teach me how to pray for *your* concerns.

Orange Juice

Jesus said to them, 'When you pray, say: "…Give us the food we need for each day." '

LUKE 11:2A,3 NCV

HAVE YOU EVER REALLY BEEN HUNGRY?

The Big Breakfast

Have you ever been *really* hungry? I mean so hungry that you might pass out because your blood sugar level is so low? For most of us, this kind of hunger usually means that, while we may have missed breakfast or lunch, we can be sure that we'll get some dinner in the next hour or two. We don't have to stop and think about where our dinner will come from. It'll be there for us every day, and that's just part of life. Aren't we fortunate?

For other people, the source of the next bite of food is not a 'given'. Our societies are still very divided between the haves and the have-nots, and for many that means their daily bread can also be a have-not.

I once read an article by a relief worker in the Sudan, who was helping people caught in a terrible famine. He told the story of a woman he saw gathering scraps from a rubbish heap. Before she or her children ate the meagre meal, she bowed her head and thanked God for the food.

Continental

Our food and everything else that keeps us alive is a gift from God. Remind yourself of this every day.

Coffee

Lord Jesus, forgive me for taking the daily food I eat for granted. Thank you for giving me what I need and more. Teach me to share.

Orange Juice
Jesus said to them, 'When you pray, say: "...Forgive us for our sins..." '

LUKE 11:2A,4A NCV

WHAT A STRANGE WORD!

The Big Breakfast
I recently heard a very well-known pop singer tell young people that if something felt right, it must be okay for them and they should go ahead and do it. 'Sin,' she said, 'is a strange word anyway! Sin isn't a word we use any more. Have you noticed? In fact, it's almost like it belongs to some foreign language.' I guess that for some it *is* a foreign language. We don't talk any more about things being a sin, which means 'wrong'. Things are neither right nor wrong: there is only choice. You choose the thing that's good for you. We've removed that word 'sin' from our dictionary.

The Bible makes a lot of things very clear. One of them is that right and wrong are not decided by us. Sin means doing wrong, and we need to ask God to forgive us when we sin.

Continental
God's ideas of right and wrong will never reach their sell-by date, because our best interest is always at the heart of them.

Coffee
Lord Jesus, help me to listen to you about what is right and wrong, and not to the popular ideas all around me.

Orange Juice

Jesus said to them, 'When you pray, say: "…Forgive us for our sins, because we forgive everyone who has done wrong to us." '

LUKE 11:2A,4 NCV

NO OPTION

The Big Breakfast

I had a mad, bad thing happen to me once. I tried to help someone who'd got himself into trouble. I thought I was helping a friend. My friendship was eventually used against me, as the person tried to get himself out of the mess he was in by denying what he'd done and putting the blame onto others, including me. I felt so let down, totally betrayed, and a real fool for having tried to help in the first place. I also discovered for the first time what it felt like to hate another human being.

When we have a wrong done against us, it usually cuts a deep wound – a wound that becomes a festering sore unless we do something to stop the rot. That something is to forgive.

When I was struggling with the pain and anger I felt, a very good friend said to me, 'Forgive. If you're a Christian, you have no option.' He was right. I had no option.

Continental

Mark Twain once said, 'Forgiveness is like a flower that has been crushed… It leaves it's fragrance on the heel of the person who stood on it.'

Coffee

Lord Jesus, I realize that you command us to forgive, and therefore we have no option. Help me to be a forgiver of wrongs for your sake as well as my own.

Orange Juice

Jesus said to them, 'When you pray, say: "… And do not cause us to be tempted."'

LUKE 11:2A,4B NCV

THE ENEMY OF THE BEST

The Big Breakfast

I'm not sure who it was who first said, 'That which seems good can often be the enemy of the best.' I reckon the things we ought not to do usually seem pretty good. In fact, they're often downright exciting. The temptation to live on the wild side can be overwhelming. That's what makes it so hard to say 'no', so hard to turn away and do the less fun thing.

At times like this we need to make a choice – a choice to go for the best, which is a choice to follow Jesus. Temptation can come to us in very obvious ways, through things we know very clearly are not what God wants. At other times, however, it can be very subtle, something that seems harmless or no big deal. Whatever the situation, the fact is that God knows we'll be tempted and so he tells us to pray. If we're bringing something to God through our prayers, it will be much harder to give in to it.

Continental

God doesn't actually create temptations and put them in our path. He sometimes allows us to be tested by them, though, which helps our faith to grow and become stronger.

Coffee

Ask God to help you recognize temptation and give you the strength to overcome it.

Orange Juice

So when you offer your gift to God at the altar, and you remember that your brother or sister has something against you, leave your gift there at the altar. Go and make peace with that person…

MATTHEW 5:23-24 NCV

DEAL WITH THE BAD STUFF

The Big Breakfast

A friend of mine upset me once. I told another friend about it, got the whole thing off my chest. Quite a few months later, the person who had upset me called and asked if we could meet for a coffee. I was happy to meet. I'd forgotten all about the incident. The first words my friend said to me, even before the coffee was poured, were, 'I'm here to ask for your forgiveness.' I was stunned. I'll never forget the impact of those words.

My friend understood something very important. It's impossible to worship God properly if we have anger in our hearts towards another person. In Matthew chapter 5, Jesus is telling his followers about the things that matter a whole lot to God. One thing God cares about a great deal is what's in our hearts, especially how we feel about other people and the attitudes that control how we feel. 'Deal with the bad stuff,' Jesus says. Unless you do, you can't worship God properly.

Continental

Ray Davey, who was a POW during the Second World War, said, 'If the Church has nothing to say about reconciliation, then the Church has nothing to say!'

Coffee

Lord Jesus, you call us to live by the values of your kingdom in everything we do. Give me the desire and the will to do it.

Orange Juice

Therefore confess your sins to each other and pray for each other so that you may be healed.

JAMES 5:16 NIV

TELLING ALL

The Big Breakfast

One of the in things right now is 'telling all' – confessing something you did to a friend as a joke, but he didn't know it was you; or some awkward situation in which you found yourself, that makes you go red just thinking about it. I've noticed that some of the teen magazines around now are getting into the tell-all habit in a big way. A while back Simon Mayo hosted a TV show that did nothing else.

I've no idea if the folk on that TV show felt healed. There *is* a place for confessing things. We need to start by telling God and asking him to forgive us. But we sometimes need to tell a buddy – a good buddy, someone who cares about us and who wants good things for us. Telling all like this can really help to sort a bad situation out. It allows us to see our mess more clearly and, if the buddy is a good one, he or she will help us face our mess and say sorry. That way we can find healing.

Continental

Get into a partnership with a friend where you can both talk honestly about your struggles and failures as Christians. It will really help you beat the bad stuff.

Coffee

Ask God to show you which of your friends could be this kind of buddy to you.

Orange Juice

And we know that in all things God works for the good of those who love him.

ROMANS 8:28 NIV

THE LONG HAUL

The Big Breakfast

When you step into the Christian faith, your life changes for ever. For one thing, absolutely everything has a meaning. God, you see, is so excited that you've given him permission to get involved in your life that he steps right in there and begins straight away to walk in you and with you. And because he has great plans for you, he gets involved in everything that comes your way.

That's the important bit to remember. He walks with you, working for you in all the life situations you might meet. How is it that we get this crazy idea that God is somehow making the kind of plans for us that take us *out* of the normal rough-and-tumble? That's not how it is. At the end of the day, God's agenda is to make sure we become like Jesus. He walks with us while we make the same journey as everybody else. The difference is, he makes the journey worth it.

Continental

God is in this for the long haul. Working for our good sometimes means that he allows us to face some very tough situations. Looking back, we can see his master plan.

Coffee

Lord Jesus, thank you that you walk with me and know how to make everything worth it.

Orange Juice

Trust the LORD with all your heart, and don't depend on your own understanding. Remember the LORD in all you do, and he will give you success.

PROVERBS 3:5–6 NCV

TRUST GOD'S WIT, NOT YOUR OWN

The Big Breakfast

I read a great story in a paper recently. A lady from outside Glasgow had driven into the city to visit a friend. She had directions to the neighbourhood, but was a bit shaky about where to go. It wasn't an area of Glasgow she knew. At one point she came to a busy road junction. The traffic lights went from red to amber to green, then back to red. In fact, they went through the cycle twice more while she tried to decide which way to turn. Eventually, the man in the car behind her got out and said, 'Lassie, do you not like the colour of any of those lights?' What a cool way to handle things!

How do you deal with big decisions – especially when any one of a number of options could be a good choice? It's a tough one. I guess that's where being a Christian makes a real difference. God promises that if we take time to get him on board, he'll help us find the right road.

Continental

The Christian faith is all about partnership between God and you. He'll help you sort things out – when you accept that your own wit isn't enough.

Coffee

Lord Jesus, thank you that the Bible is packed full of great promises from you and God.

Orange Juice

…a person who hates being corrected is stupid… the wise listen to advice.

PROVERBS 12:1B,15B NCV

THE 'MOST EXCELLENT ADVICE' BOOK

The Big Breakfast

I know a man who will never accept that he's made a mistake. It's just amazing to watch. Even if his mistake is a genuine slip-up, he wriggles and squirms, trying to make himself out to be Mr Innocent. It's become a standing joke. David (not his real name) is truly Mr 'I Never Make A Mistake'! The sad thing, of course, is that nobody takes him seriously any more.

I love the way the Bible is full of such excellent advice. Look at this proverb: you're stupid if you don't let other people tell you when you're getting it wrong; you're smart when you listen to good advice. What could be simpler? Yet for some of us, it seems, such advice is so hard to follow.

Continental

Why would someone not want to take advice? Nobody gets everything right. Could it be that old devil called pride again?

Coffee

There are a few things that God hates with a passion. Pride is one of them. Think about it.

Orange Juice
Careless words stab like a sword, but wise words bring healing.

PROVERBS 12:18 NCV

THE SHOW MUST GO ON

The Big Breakfast
Have you watched much of that confessional TV stuff? You know the kind of thing. Two sisters haven't talked for a year. One of them comes on and talks about it in front of a live audience. The other sister is listening backstage. She's not too thrilled about what's being said about her. Eventually the two sisters are sitting there together, sorting it out in front of the whole world. The show will get a higher rating if the sisters have a good go at one another. Words that stab like a sword.

Sometimes our words can be intentionally cruel because we feel hurt, let down or betrayed. We deal with our pain by hurting another person. Sometimes we use cruel words because we feel threatened, jealous or maybe a little less important than someone else. Sometimes we're just plain careless.

As followers of Jesus, every word we speak is important. Our words should never stab like a sword, because that destroys. Rather, we should look for ways to build people up. Wise words are good for building up.

Continental
Are there times you look back to and wish you could cut out your tongue, because of something you said? Remember, wise words bring healing.

Coffee
Lord Jesus, please prompt me before I open my mouth, so that I speak words that build people up rather than stab them in the heart.

Orange Juice

A gentle answer will calm a person's anger, but an unkind answer will cause more anger.

PROVERBS 15:1 NCV

WAR OF WORDS

The Big Breakfast

It was a war zone. That was what it was like. The missiles were vicious. They cut to a ribbon in seconds. Neither side would give in.

What does that sound like? You and your sister having a row over a new shirt you bought that she wore first? Some of the politicians who are supposed to be running our country having a ratings battle in the run-up to an election?

I started to follow Jesus when I was 16. It was a very clear thing for me. I knew he wanted me to follow him and live by his guidelines. Why couldn't I do it, then, when my sister had a go at me? She seemed to know how to press that button and off I'd go, yelling at her as loudly as she yelled at me. It got me down. One day I found this verse in Proverbs. I began to put it into practice. It wasn't always easy. I really wanted to yell back. God helped me not to, however, and my sister and I became very good friends.

Continental

Kindness and gentleness aren't difficult. They just take practice.

Coffee

Lord Jesus, I want to be your follower in everything I do. Help me to remember that includes the words I speak.

Orange Juice

A friend loves you all the time, and a brother helps in times of trouble.

PROVERBS 17:17 NCV

NO. 1 BECOMES NO. 2

The Big Breakfast

Matt, Lisa, David, Matthew, Courtney and Jennifer got a pay rise a while ago. They now receive a cool $750,000 each for every episode they make of the hit TV sitcom *Friends*. That's some fee. There's something else that's impressive about these six performers, and it's not how good they are at making us laugh. It's their friendship off screen as well as on. Apparently they've made a pact with one another about when it's time to quit the show. If one goes, they all go.

There isn't a lot of that kind of commitment around these days. It's good to see it now and again. The wise words from Proverbs gives it to us straight. Be a true friend – be someone who cares for their buddies all the time, someone who knows how to be committed, to be there, to hang in there, no matter what. That's a true friend. That's what it means to love at all times.

Continental

There's a serious pressure on us today to look out only for No. 1. The kind of friend the Bible calls for means that No. 1 becomes No. 2.

Coffee

Lord Jesus, show me today what my friends really need from me and how I can be there for them.

Orange Juice

Your word is a lamp to my feet and a light for my path.

PSALM 119:105 NIV

READ IT RIGHT

The Big Breakfast

A friend rang me in a bit of a state the other day. Her best friend had just dropped a bombshell. She was leaving her husband to go and live with someone else. Her husband was a good man. He'd always been kind and they were good friends, but she didn't love him any more. She did love the other person. My friend was devastated. The couple whose marriage was about to get blown into a million pieces was one of the few Christian partnerships she admired. The most upsetting thing of all was the way her friend used the Bible to justify what she was about to do. 'God's okay with this,' she said.

The Bible is the best way to discover what God is really saying, through his clear guidelines for us. We do need to read it properly, however, and that takes patience and practice. Then we'll discover that it's much more than a rule book. It's a wonderful revelation of God and all he wants for us, which is very good indeed.

Continental

We don't apply our lives to the Bible. We apply the Bible to our lives. Think about the difference, then go and do it.

Coffee

Lord Jesus, I confess that I sometimes find the Bible hard to understand. Please help me, and show me how to help myself.

Orange Juice

'The LORD has left me; the LORD has forgotten me.' The LORD answers, 'Can a woman forget the baby she nurses? ... Even if she could forget her children, I will not forget you. See, I have written your name on my hand.'

ISAIAH 49:14–16 NCV

GIFT-WRAPPED ANSWERS

The Big Breakfast

I read a comment recently which was made by a Christian person who was having a tough time:

'I am sick of Christians offering me gift-wrapped answers when my world is falling apart.'

How is your world today? Did you jump out of bed full of energy, skip to the bathroom, dash downstairs for coffee and orange juice and run out into the sunshine excited about what lay ahead of you? You did? What kind of coffee do you drink? I want some!

Or did your day start with a heavy black cloud hovering over you, your feet like lead, your heart so sore that you feel you'll never be free from the pain?

It may be that both of these pictures are way too dramatic. You're neither elated nor in despair. Our lives do have highs and lows, however, and everything in between. It's part of the deal. What doesn't feel like part of the deal is God's silence during the dark and cloudy days. It's at times like these that we need him most, so how come it feels as if he's away on vacation?

Continental

Part of our growing as Christians can only happen in the dark place where God appears to have abandoned us. In these moments, trust what you *know* of God, not what you feel.

Coffee

Your name is written on the palm of God's hand. It's impossible for him to forget you.

Orange Juice

While they were talking and discussing, Jesus himself came near and began walking with them.

LUKE 24:15 NCV

A SUNDAY-SCHOOL JESUS

The Big Breakfast

When I first met her she weighed 17 stone, but her face was one of the prettiest I had ever seen. She had wonderful, deep brown eyes, a complexion to die for and the neatest mouth. But the black, black shadows under her engaging eyes dominated that beautiful face. I knew there was a story that needed to be heard, to be told to someone who would listen and understand.

I walked with Jennifer for hundreds of miles. It took us 10 years. Recently she said the most fantastic thing: 'I feel I have at last come out of a dark jungle and the best bit is, I've realized Jesus has been beside me all the time, listening to everything you and I have talked about.' As I looked at her beautiful face, I was overcome. This girl had come from a place of darkness that I couldn't begin to understand. The memory of a Sunday-school Jesus had brought her through the door of our youth centre one day – and the rest is history.

Continental

In Luke chapter 24 there's a fantastic account of Jesus walking beside two very broken people. He listened, he understood, and his presence transformed their lives.

Coffee

Jesus didn't come to remove the painful parts of life. He came to stand with us, to listen and understand us, and to transform our lives.

Orange Juice

To the Jews who had believed him, Jesus said, 'If you hold to my teaching, you are really my disciples. Then you will know the truth, and the truth will set you free.'

JOHN 8:31–32 NIV

WALK THE WALK

The Big Breakfast

Let's go back for a moment to Morpheus and Neo in *The Matrix*. Here's Morpheus again: 'There's a difference between knowing the path and walking the path.' Jesus and Morpheus both have this right, don't they? Jesus is telling people to follow what he tells them. Why? Because his words will give them what they need to get it right. To get what right? The way to live, of course.

Morpheus has got a few things sussed out. You can acquire the knowledge, but you need to walk the path to make that knowledge any use. Jesus has explained that acquiring the knowledge from him is a start, but you then have to walk the path. By that he means you have to live by the good things he's told you. Do it his way, and you'll be free.

I wonder what he means by 'free'? My guess is that Jesus is letting us know that in our lives we'll come across many ways to live which seem good, but his way is the only one that guarantees us good choices.

Continental

I get very sad as I listen to some of the song lyrics around today. Popping pills to get rid of the pain is a theme that comes up too often. If only people would look to Jesus.

Coffee

Just as Morpheus does for Neo, Jesus has shown us the path. We must make the choice to walk it. That's a choice we need to make every day.

Orange Juice

God does not see the same way people see. People look at the outside of a person, but the LORD looks at the heart.

1 SAMUEL 16:7B NCV

THE YEAR I WAS 16

The Big Breakfast

I was speaking once to a class of 80 high-school girls. What a fantastic group they were. Energetic and peachy-faced, they reminded me of those crazy days of falling in love one moment and wondering where your eyesight was the next ... the war with acne, with parents or teachers, and with all those other stupid people who seemed to be out of the Dark Ages ... the discoveries that belonged only to 'the year I was 16'.

I smiled to myself. Most of it had a familiar feel – except for one thing. They were all on a diet. Yes, all of them. I couldn't believe it. The whole 'I'm too fat/too thin' routine in itself was no surprise. It goes with the territory of being 16. To find a *whole* year group deeply unhappy with how they looked, however, was just terrible. I looked around that schoolroom and wanted to weep. They were beautiful, absolutely lovely, but they felt ugly. Who had filled their heads with such a lie?

Continental

We all want to be beautiful, to have a face that's our passport to acceptance. God means it when he tells us that what we are on the inside is much more important.

Coffee

Inner perfection glows. People see it on your face. It gives a beauty that never fades, that draws people to you because you're good to be around.

Orange Juice

I will go to the king, even though it is against the law. And if I perish, I perish.

ESTHER 4:16B NIV

DOING WHAT JESUS WOULD DO

The Big Breakfast

I bought the *Big Issue* from a boy from Kosovo one day. He was standing in the middle of the road in the rush hour, taking advantage of the red traffic light. I wondered how many he'd sold that day. It was pouring with rain.

My *Big Issue* contained an article about asylum seekers. That seemed ironic because of the boy from Kosovo. The article was very depressing, except for one brief extract. A journalist wrote about a busload of asylum seekers who were looking scared and deeply dejected. She decided to risk giving them a wave and a thumbs-up, despite the hostility of those around her. Instantly the scared faces on the bus broke into smiles and expressions of gratitude.

The story in the Bible that surrounds this verse from Esther is about a race of people in a strange country. They were under incredible threat. The courage of a young girl who was prepared to take a risk that could have cost her life saved thousands of people.

Continental

Following Jesus means coming at life from a completely different direction from those people who don't follow him. Our priority is to do what Jesus would do in every situation.

Coffee

Lord Jesus, you may not ask me to risk my life for you, but help me to take the kind of risks that will make a difference for other people, as well as honouring you.

Orange Juice

And who knows, you may have been chosen queen for just such a time as this.

ESTHER 4:14B NCV

HALT THE EVIL MOMENT

The Big Breakfast

The right place at the right time. When we follow Jesus, there are a million times in our lives when we'll be in the right place at the right time. We're his hands and his feet. We're his messengers, passing on his story to others around us. We need to realize that where we are today, the people we spend time with and the opportunities that come our way are in a strange way organized by him. Jesus works in us and through us to impact the world around us – even though we don't quite know how he does it!

God really cares about the world he made. He hates to see people ignore him and do things their own way. It leads to injustice, to broken people and broken communities, to violence and death. As people who follow Jesus, we're strategically placed to bring his fragrance into every situation. It's a fragrance that has power to halt an evil moment. Esther was chosen to be queen for such a moment. She halted a Jewish holocaust long before Hitler was around.

Continental

We want our world to be a place where people do good things to one another. We know it isn't. Today you are where you are so that God can reach in and halt evil.

Coffee

Lord Jesus, use me today to make a difference right in the place where you've placed me.

Orange Juice

Jesus said to her, 'I am the resurrection and the life. Those who believe in me will have life even if they die.'

JOHN 11:25 NCV

DON'T MENTION THE 'D' WORD

The Big Breakfast

'I feel strongly that death does not exist.' Those are the words from a recent interview with Brian Blessed, the actor and explorer who undertook a climb up Everest in 1993. I was intrigued by the way he thought about death. For him it was the next phase in life, a place to move on to that would eventually bring him back to where he'd started.

Do you ever think about death? I guess not. It seems a long way off, so why get upset about it? Unless, that is, you've already been forced to feel its painful effects through the loss of a close friend or member of your family. Death upsets us. Relationships and friendships that matter a lot get interrupted by death, and very often we simply don't understand why.

Jesus has been there. He has made it through death. He doesn't take away the pain of being separated from someone special. He does make sense of it, though, because he gives meaning to the other side of death.

Continental

Jesus is the only person who can make sense of death, because he's the only person to have beaten it. Ask him to help you understand what that means.

Coffee

Lord Jesus, I don't think about death. It scares me. Show me what it means to believe in you and to have life even if I die.

Orange Juice

...but Mary stood outside the tomb crying ... Jesus said to her, 'Mary.'

JOHN 20:11,16 NIV

I DIDN'T GET TO SAY GOODBYE

The Big Breakfast

A few years ago, I had a phone call very early one morning. My brother's voice was broken and thick with tears. The next few seconds were agony. His news was clearly going to be bad. 'Oh God, will I be able to cope? Will I handle it? What if I can't deal with it?'

My Dad had died suddenly of a heart attack.

'Please God, tell me why. Why him? He was so young. Too young. I didn't get to say goodbye. I can't cope. I can't take this. I don't know how to handle this. I don't know how to lose him, how to exist without him. Oh God, don't you know he was such good fun? He was the big guy in our family. We all needed him. We still need him. Why? Why? Why?'

Then God spoke my name. In the middle of that moment of insanity, he spoke my name. My Dad was safe. He was with Jesus. My heart was absolutely broken, shattered to pieces, but my soul was at peace.

Continental

The journey we must take can be desperately difficult at times. Jesus doesn't take us out of the really painful moments. He makes sense of them.

Coffee

Lord Jesus, I wish there was some knack to grief, but I know there isn't. Thank you that in the middle of such pain you have something personal to say to us.

Orange Juice
You will be my witnesses – in Jerusalem, in all of Judea, in Samaria and in every part of the world.

ACTS 1:8B NCV

MAY THE FORCE BE WITH YOU

The Big Breakfast
When you know Jesus and how important it is to have him in your life, how do you tell others?

This is a question with which many of us struggle. Everybody seems to have their own answer to what it means to find spiritual togetherness. Richard Gere, we're told, wears something called a 'spirituality bracelet'. It reminds him of the inner peace he's searching for. Then there's the command, 'Don't think, feel – and may the Force be with you,' given by Liam Neeson as the Jedi Qui-Gon in the movie *Star Wars: The Phantom Menace*. Spiritual matters are really important to many people. There's a big search on for the spiritual path or journey that will fill the inner gap, and every week some new experience is promoted. If only Jesus could be seen more clearly.

Well, that's our job. I recently read a great quote from a church pastor: 'When the world doesn't know what to believe, we need to stand up and tell them God's story in a way they'll be sure to get it.'

Continental
God's story is about loving people unconditionally. Our friends will understand the story a whole lot better if we love them unconditionally.

Coffee
Lord Jesus, give me your heart for those around me who don't know you, and help me to serve them for your sake.

Orange Juice
...but I came to give life – life in all its fullness.

JOHN 10:10 NCV

WHAT IF?

The Big Breakfast
What if things were going well for me, so well that I hardly believed it would last? Close friends who were always there for me; a family I was proud to be part of; a Mum and Dad who made me feel good about myself, who just knew that sometimes I didn't understand what was going on in my head, but said that was okay. What if now I could see that I hadn't understood how special it was to have a Mum and Dad like that? I'd done the drugs and free-love thing, or just ignored them in preference for my friends. What if?

What if life at home had been a nightmare? What if Mum and Dad had been so busy tearing one another apart that they'd failed to notice I was losing it at school? What if home was a place of terror not safety, a place where I dreaded going to sleep at night – the footsteps on the stairs, the presence in my room and those dreaded words, 'This is our secret…'? What if?

Continental
What if God was able to help us make sense of everything that was going on in our heads, able to lead us to a place of healing and wholeness? What if?

Coffee
When Jesus gives us his life, we can sing as if we're in the shower, dance as if no one is watching and love as if we've never been hurt.

Orange Juice
Honour your father and your mother so that you will live a long time in the land that the LORD your God is going to give you.

EXODUS 20:12 NCV

I JUST DON'T LOVE HER

The Big Breakfast
This thing about honouring your parents: it's pretty easy, isn't it? Certainly, they get on our nerves from time to time, nagging about a tidy bedroom, a clean and respectable appearance, good table manners, getting a good job, and so on. But they're not a bad pair really, as parents go. So if God wants them honoured, that's fine.

Well, for some of us it's not fine, not that easy. A good friend said to me recently about his mother: 'I just don't love her, so how can I honour her? But God says I must.' This wasn't just a 'shrug the shoulders and get on with it' kind of comment. He was having a truly bad time about it. His mother had been emotionally abusive to him all his life, especially through his growing-up years. He'd promised himself that he would never allow hate to creep in. Now, though, he neither loved nor hated. He felt nothing. I didn't know all the ins and outs of this relationship. What I did know, however, was that he regularly went to visit her. He sent her birthday cards. So actually he *was* honouring her. It just didn't feel like it.

Continental
The painful experiences that happen to us sometimes seem to make God's commandments look impossible. They're not. We just need to allow him to show us how to go about it.

Coffee
Lord Jesus, I'm slowly realizing that to do what you command sometimes means that my head and my heart haven't quite caught up with one another. Help me to do what you want me to, no matter how I feel.

Orange Juice

Then Jesus used this story to teach his followers that they should always pray and never lose hope.

LUKE 18:1 NCV

DOING SOMETHING PRACTICAL

The Big Breakfast

Jesus is telling his followers to take prayer seriously. Do it all the time. No excuses, just keep praying. That's his message. Is that how things are for you? I imagine that, if you're anything like the rest of us, prayer often gets squeezed out by things that seem more important. Or perhaps prayer itself doesn't make much sense. Doing something practical would seem to make a lot *more* sense.

Perhaps we come to our senses when the important matters in our lives just can't be sorted out by doing something practical. Jesus has a very clear message. Pray all the time. Pray about everything that's happening in your life. Pray when you're happy. Pray when you're sad. Pray when you're in trouble, afraid, lonely, struggling to make sense of your life. Pray, and don't give up.

The story Jesus goes on to tell shows us how prayer makes a difference when we're in trouble. Pray all the time, but especially when there's a problem that needs sorting.

Continental

Praying when we're in trouble can be a desperate struggle. Don't give up hope. Jesus says that things do change when you pray. Ask people in South Africa or Northern Ireland.

Coffee

'Is anything too hard for the LORD?' (Genesis 18:14)

Orange Juice
In a certain town there was a judge who did not respect God or care about people.

LUKE 18:2 NCV

SURVIVAL OF THE FITTEST

The Big Breakfast
When we come to read the Bible, we need to remember that the whole story God wants us to hear will really only make sense when we read the whole book. All 66 books will take us the whole way, just like the highway Interstate 66 in the USA.

The followers listening to Jesus as he told this story in Luke 18 would have understood what he was getting at because they'd been on the Interstate, so to speak. They would have known that the job of a judge was to act as God's representative, and therefore he was expected to be 100 per cent honest and fair. He was there to care for people, to look out for them, to make sure the weak and vulnerable were looked after, that the underprivileged got a just deal. Under no circumstances was he ever to take a bribe or be corrupted by another human being (see 2 Chronicles 19:4–6). A judge who didn't respect God and who didn't care for people was a sign of huge trouble. It would have been no surprise, however. Corruption was expected. The bribe was normal. It was another case of the survival of the fittest.

Continental
In many countries today the people with the power to protect and care for people can't be trusted. Bribery is common. The result is that ordinary people never get justice.

Coffee
Part of our job as Christians is to fight for the rights of those who can't fight for themselves. How could you play your part in this fight?

Orange Juice
In that same town there was a widow who kept coming to this judge, saying, 'Give me my rights against my enemy.'

LUKE 18:3 NCV

WEAR YOUR
GOD-GLASSES

The Big Breakfast
Who are the people without a voice in our society? Who has no rights? Name them to yourself now. Jewish society knew that there were people who needed protecting. The widow was one such person. She was a pretty defenceless person. She had no man to fight for her rights. Remember the restrictions on women then: they could only appear and speak in public if they had a man with them. A lone woman without powerful men friends was in a difficult situation. Jewish law, however, stated that the widow was to be heard. She had legal rights because of her desolate state (see Isaiah 1:17).

The widow in Jesus' story wasn't having her rights recognized. She'd come again and again to this judge. She probably had no money, so she couldn't pay a bribe, which was the usual way to get your case heard. To make matters worse for her, 'the enemy' she complained of probably *had* paid a bribe. The law that should have been protecting her was letting her down instead.

Continental
The whole point of the story is that justice is absent. God hates injustice. As Christians we should actively challenge injustice. The problem is, we often fail to see it. We don't wear our 'God-glasses'.

Coffee
One way to be God's voice against injustice in our society is to actively lobby the government and push for God-honouring laws. This takes courage.

Orange Juice

… the judge refused to help her. But afterwards, he thought to himself, 'Even though I don't respect God or care about people, I will see that she gets her rights. Otherwise she will continue to bother me until I am worn out.'

LUKE 18:4–5 NCV

NEVER GIVE UP

The Big Breakfast

This poor woman: she has no money, so she can't pay a bribe; she has no man in her life to fight for her. She has only one way out. All she can do is to keep pleading, no matter how hopeless the situation seems, hoping to wear the judge down.

The judge says of himself that he's corrupt. He can't be shamed into doing what's right. He doesn't care what people think of him. And as for God, well, he has no fear of God either.

What does the story have to say to us? I think it's something like this. Keep praying. Keep coming to God with your requests. Be persistent. If a corrupt judge is eventually worn down by the pleading of a widow, how much more likely it is that God – who is loving, kind, compassionate and just – will answer you and help you.

Continental

Prayer is a mystery. It isn't about 'wish lists', nor is it about changing God's mind. That would be to misunderstand Jesus. It's about bringing genuine need to God and not giving up.

Coffee

Perhaps the key is to remember that we come to a loving Father, not a twisted judge. His response to our prayers can always be trusted.

Orange Juice
The Lord said, 'Listen to what the unfair judge said. God will always give what is right to his people who cry to him night and day, and he will not be slow to answer them.'

LUKE 18:6–7 NCV

PRAYER IS AN ADVENTURE

The Big Breakfast
When Jesus talked about 'his people', i.e. God's people, the disciples would immediately have thought of the family of Israel. We can read all about them in the Old Testament. Jesus was saying that God would give them what was right and good when they prayed.

This is quite amazing. Stop and think for a moment who we're talking about. You know them: they're on every page of the Old Testament, trying God's patience to the limit, never seeming to get it right, even when it was obvious what they should do. They had sign after sign of God's goodness, and still they ran off at the first sight of trouble! It gives us hope, doesn't it? God never gave up on them.

The Old Testament is an incredible story of God's involvement in the real world of real people. He suffered with them and cared for them, teaching them how to live. He stuck with them, even if at times he had to allow them to go through hard times. He knew that was the only way they would ever come to their senses.

Continental
God was angry many times with his people, threatening to give up on them. He couldn't, though. Just as he can't give up on us, especially if we pray.

Coffee
Prayer is an adventure. Through prayer, we recognize that God is good, that he cares, but also that his way is the right one.

Orange Juice
But when the Son of Man comes again, will he find those on earth who believe in him?

LUKE 18:8B NCV

PRAYER AND FAITH TOGETHER

The Big Breakfast
Prayer and faith go together. What is faith? That's a hard question. We've all heard those silly stories about chairs holding us up and 'faith' being the fact that we believe in the chair! I don't know about you, but that kind of explanation never helped me to understand faith.

I read a helpful comment recently: 'God is the focus of our faith, the purifier of our faith and the provider of faith's longings' (Charles Ringma, *Resist the Powers*, Albatross Books).

(1) God is the focus of our faith. Get to know God. Know about him. Know him as a great friend and as someone who wants to know you in return. Faith will become natural, as God becomes your Father.

(2) God will purify our faith. We need help to develop a faith that's based on reality not fairy tales. God isn't a genie in a lamp, or a heavenly Santa Claus. We often behave as if he is! God will purify our faith. Be prepared. That's usually painful.

Continental
When Jesus returns, will he find faith on earth? Don't be fooled into believing that faith in God is outdated. Like the Old Testament people, we will discover that such a notion is pure deception. Jesus is for today!

Coffee
Lord Jesus, I want my faith to grow. I don't want to disappoint you. Please give me faith when I'm tempted to doubt.

Orange Juice
However, when the Son of Man comes, will he find faith on the earth?

LUKE 18:8 NIV

JESUS: THE TRUE SOURCE

The Big Breakfast
Faith isn't about how we feel. This is hard to take in. 'If it feels right, do it.' You've probably heard that a lot recently. Don't misunderstand me: how we feel is very important. God made us body, mind and spirit. Jesus honours our wholeness when he tells us to love God with all of who we are – our heart (emotions), mind (intellect), soul (spirit) and strength (physical body). Sometimes, though, our mind or our understanding must lead the way. Getting to know God well will make that a great deal easier.

Being a follower of Jesus, which means having faith in him and God, isn't just about our own wants and needs. It's also about other people. Jesus asks if he'll find faith on earth. I guess he wants to know if those who say they're his followers are actually getting on with the job – the kingdom job of fighting injustice, speaking out on God's good and pure ways to live, and telling the world how important it is to honour him. Will the Son of Man find faith on earth?

Continental
Maybe faith isn't the most difficult bit. Crystals, palm readings, special bracelets – these all need 'faith' in order to work. Seeing Jesus as the true source of faith – now that's a whole lot harder.

Coffee
Lord Jesus, I'm beginning to understand that by doing things that demonstrate my faith in you I'll show others where true faith is found.

Orange Juice
We have this treasure from God, but we are like clay jars that hold the treasure. This shows that the great power is from God, not from us.

2 CORINTHIANS 4:7 NCV

THE START-UP GROUP

The Big Breakfast
If Jesus had sent the profiles of his 12 disciples to a management consultant and asked for an opinion on his choice of recruits, what do you think the response would have been? 'You're off your trolley, Jesus! This lot are a complete disaster. Peter doesn't know how to control his temper, nor does he have any natural wit. Matthew comes with a very poor reputation. I wouldn't have him in your start-up group. Much too risky … You do have one good one. He's good with money, he's astute, he understands that strategy is important. Yes, I'd keep Judas Iscariot and get rid of the rest!'

Jesus, of course, would have ignored such advice. It was those 11 original disciples (minus Judas) who started the Christian Church. Since then, millions and millions of people have joined. It's estimated that throughout the world every day, 63,000 people become Christians and 1,600 churches are planted.

Continental
We're like jars of clay that break easily. Jesus doesn't have his eye on strength and ability when he's looking for disciples. Rather, he's looking for a willing jar to carry his message.

Coffee
Lord Jesus, it's amazing to think that those unlikely disciples were your start-up group. I'm no different, yet you choose to use me too. Thank you.

Orange Juice

The devil who rules this world has blinded the minds of those who do not believe. They cannot see the light of the Good News.

2 CORINTHIANS 4:4 NCV

EXPOSE THIS LIE

The Big Breakfast

We live in a world of lies. Satan, the devil, the evil opposer of God and his kingdom, is alive and well. He blinds people. He's been at it for a long time. In the very beginning it was Satan who told Adam and Eve that they'd be okay if they ignored what God told them and did their own thing.

Are you aware of some of his big lies today? The latest cool, trendy thing that promises to 'make life a blast'. The idea that wearing great gear will solve your image problem. The pressure never to be without a boy/girl partner, because that will sort the need to belong. The idea that good sex will solve the search for love.

Who's he kidding? Who are we kidding? Great gear is wonderful, but it won't change how we feel inside. A loving relationship is a great gift and sex in the right context is enormously special, but belonging runs much deeper than that. We live in this sea of lies every day. Satan must laugh out loud at times. Our job, those of us who follow Jesus, is to expose his lies.

Continental

Expose the lies of Satan by speaking God's truth in every situation. Satan is enjoying a free rule because of our silence.

Coffee

Lord Jesus, I'm not always sure how to speak your truth in the situations in which I find myself. Please show me how.

Orange Juice
But we have turned away from secret and shameful ways. We use no trickery, and we do not change the teaching of God.

2 CORINTHIANS 4:2 NCV

GOD GOES ONLINE

The Big Breakfast
Well, there's www.beliefnet.com, www.gospel.com.net, www.spiritchannel.com and www.ibelieve.com. God has gone online. Websites are now available for the ever-growing numbers of net-surfers looking for answers to religious questions. An estimated 600,000 sites exist (and this figure doesn't include home pages for churches and religious organizations or groups). A recent survey suggested that a quarter of all net-surfers have visited sites for religious purposes. Apparently this makes it as popular a subject as sex!

This is great news. The hunger for spiritual answers gives us, as followers of Jesus, a wonderful opportunity to tell people about him. For a change we'll be answering the questions they're asking. There's an interesting warning in this verse from 2 Corinthians, however. As we share God's story with people, we must do it openly. We must be up-front and honest in speaking the truth God has given us without changing any of it. That's not always easy, because some of God's truth can be offensive to people. We need to tell it as it is, nonetheless.

Continental
The gospel, God's story, is his story not ours. We must tell it as it is and allow God to deal with the consequences.

Coffee
Lord Jesus, sometimes it's tempting to tell people what they want to hear rather than the truths you show us in your word. Help me to avoid that temptation.

Orange Juice

If you love me, you will obey my commands. I will ask the Father, and he will give you another Helper to be with you for ever – the Spirit of truth.

JOHN 14:15 NCV

FROM FRIEND TO BROTHER

The Big Breakfast

Do you remember how tough it was to get your maths homework done? If calculus and trigonometry weren't your thing, it was total torture with no way out. Maths was one of those subjects everybody had to pass. It was always great when a friend who understood it better gave you some help.

The Holy Spirit is a bit like that friend. Firstly, he *is* a friend, a really good friend. He's there to help, especially as we try to understand all the things Jesus taught. The Holy Spirit will help us make sense of it, and will remind us about it as time goes on.

His job is bigger than that, though. He reveals Jesus himself to us, and to those who don't believe. As he does that, he shows very clearly what sin is, and also shows that sin (living for ourselves not God) has consequences. I guess that's the link shown in this verse. Jesus says that if we love him, we will obey him. The Holy Spirit will teach us about Jesus and help us to love him.

Continental

'We took off as pilots, we flew as friends and we came home as brothers.' This is Brian Jones, the round-the-world balloonist, talking about his co-pilot Bertrand.

Coffee

The Holy Spirit will stick with us the whole way, first as our friend and then as our brother.

Orange Juice

And this is eternal life: that people know you, the only true God, and that they know Jesus Christ, the One you sent.

JOHN 17:3 NCV

THE BIG-TIME SEARCH

The Big Breakfast

A survey of internet users recently revealed that a quarter of all surfers have used the net for religious purposes. Sites offer religious instruction on how to raise your child, or how to read the Bible, and there's even one offering users an online confessional box. Of enormous interest is the question, 'Is there eternal life?' People want to know, 'What happens when we die, and can we be sure God won't let us down on that one?'

Eternal life is about knowing God now – today, while we're still alive. It's not about 'pie in the sky when I die'. How is it that we've missed that? Everyone's looking for real life. This explosion of interest on the internet is only one piece of evidence for that. The search for spiritual meaning is on, big time.

Jesus tells us through this special prayer that knowing him and knowing God now, as well as after we die, is what life is all about. Why are we keeping this amazing truth to ourselves? It was never meant to be the best-kept secret in the world.

Continental

Have you noticed how many new religions there are around today? Jesus makes it clear that he is the way, the truth and the life (John 14:6).

Coffee

Jesus knows that our friends won't always understand why we want to know and follow him. That's why he promised to pray for us (John 17:9).

Orange Juice
Stop judging by the way things look, but judge by what is really right.

JOHN 7:24 NCV

X-RATINGS

The Big Breakfast
The potato and avocado salad was the star dish. Everyone was raving about it. Why? Jamie Oliver, who made cooking cool, was the reason. It was just one of many sexy cook-ups from his popular TV series. How is it that good old potato salad with a bit of avocado thrown in gets to be sexy? And that's not all that gets the x-rating these days – shoes, furniture, cars, breakfast television … even kitchen weighing scales can be dubbed 'sexy'!

If the image is right, it'll be a runaway success. The cosmetic companies are onto this as well. Courtney Thorne Smith (alias Georgia from *Ally McBeal*) is Almay's new cover girl, Cindy Crawford is selling Foster Grant sunglasses and Shania Twain is reportedly $5 million better off thanks to Revlon ColorStay.

How is it that we still get caught up with 'image'? God isn't impressed. He's much more interested in what's going on inside, in the state of our hearts and minds.

Continental
Brigitte Bardot said, 'I am what I am. I have wrinkles. Even if I had a face-lift, what about the marks etched by life on the heart and soul? You can't get those lifted.'

Coffee
Lord Jesus, the pressure to follow the in-crowd is all around me. Help me to step aside, to listen for your perspective and follow your lead.

Orange Juice
Be still, and know that I am God.

PSALM 46:10 NIV

BE STILL: SETTLE YOURSELF

The Big Breakfast
Nothing manages to be unhurried these days. We buy a cappuccino to go. There isn't time to drink it in the café. We wish we had 30 hours in every day, 8 days in every week and 20 months in every year. There's never enough time.

God says, 'Be still and know me.' Stop all this crazy running around. None of it matters as much as you think. Have the courage to stop dead, now, and have a good long look at yourself.

There's a great story in the New Testament about this kind of busyness. Mary and Martha have invited Jesus to dinner. Martha runs around the place getting everything prepared, while Mary simply sits and listens to Jesus. You can just imagine Martha's tone when she's had enough of being the kitchen slave. 'Lord, don't you care that my sister has left me alone to do all the work? Tell her to help me!' (see Luke 10:40).

'Be still,' God says. The most important thing is to take time with God. The rest will fall into place.

Continental
We were created for a relationship with God and with one another. How come our lives have got so out of control that there's time for neither?

Coffee
Lord Jesus, I know I'm far too busy, that I squeeze you and other people into second place. Forgive me, and help me to change.

Orange Juice

You are God's children whom he loves, so try to be like him. Live a life of love just as Christ loved us and gave himself for us as a sweet-smelling offering and sacrifice to God.

EPHESIANS 5:1 NCV

INSIDE OUT

The Big Breakfast

Paul makes a strong statement here. 'Be like God.' The NIV translation says 'be imitators of God'. Does this mean that we should be mimics, like Rory Bremner? No, because that's a copycat, sometimes mocking form of imitation. We're called not to copy God, but to allow him to transform us from the inside out, so that we become like him almost without knowing it. 'Let Christ be formed in you' is another way of expressing this. Then we'll be living the life of love that God has planned for us.

The mission of Jesus was to bring about a new way of living, one that's driven by love. What does that mean? I guess it means that we come to understand the shift from religion to relationship. No longer is faith just a rule-book existence or merely a philosophy for living. It's a transformed life that comes out of a dynamic relationship with Jesus.

Continental

John Lennon sang, 'All you need is love...' He was right. All you need is the love of God transforming everything you are and everything you do.

Coffee

Lord Jesus, come round my way today. Please work your transforming love in my life, so that I can be like you and love like you.

Orange Juice
In Christ we can come before God with freedom and without fear.

EPHESIANS 3:12 NCV

WHAT'S IN A NAME?

The Big Breakfast
It's all down to Jesus. Do you see that? In him, through faith in him, we can approach God.

That's awesome. We've lost some of the wonder that ought to grip us when we read a verse like this. First-century Jews were in such awe of God, in such fear of him, that they wouldn't use his name. The very idea that they could approach him in freedom and confidence was something they could not have imagined.

Life in the Spirit, the new order Jesus has brought about for us, is about discovering how incredible the love of God is. It's a love we can discover through faith in Jesus, and only Jesus. What sets Christianity apart from all other religions? It's the *relationship* we can have with the living God. That's what it's all about. It isn't a philosophy, or a way of thinking. It's a friendship with the greatest person ever.

Continental
What would it mean to you if Prince William, the heir to the British throne, wanted to be your friend? You might be awestruck by such an idea. Friendship with God is much bigger than that.

Coffee
Lord, I haven't understood the real meaning of this verse at all. Forgive me. Please give me a sense of it today and an understanding of what it cost you.

Orange Juice

I pray that Christ will live in your hearts by faith and that your lives will be strong in love and be built on love.

EPHESIANS 3:17 NCV

THE LIFE THAT'S DIFFERENT

The Big Breakfast

If the outworking of God's love in us is absent, then we haven't spent enough time with him. To train or push ourselves to be good, caring, genuine people is to miss the point. We're all created in his image, so everyone will show something of him. Gentleness, kindness, compassion – these are the kind of attributes we admire and hope to find in people. They're there in every human being because every human being shows something of God, our creator.

The fruit of the Spirit is different. It's the life and love of God, formed in us and shared through us. This is hard to grasp. What is our part? What do we have to do so that this will come about? Well, nothing. Nothing, that is, except spend time with him, and determine to allow nothing to get in the way of our relationship with him. Jesus didn't go through the horrors of the cross to produce a new variety of rule-book Christian. He faced Golgotha because he wanted people who would show the world what he's like.

Continental

Let's stop 'doing' the Christian life. Step aside and allow God to *be* the Christian life through you. Then you will love as he loves.

Coffee

The focus of Christianity is God, not ourselves.

Orange Juice

With God's power working in us, God can do much, much more than anything we can ask or imagine.

EPHESIANS 3:20 NCV

The Big Breakfast

The power that's at work in us is the same power that raised Jesus from the dead. Ephesians 1:20 tells us this. Now that's incredible. What kind of power is it that can raise a person from the dead? This is the awesome power which is only found in the living God.

As you think about this today, do you get just a tiny feeling that something might be missing? Where is this kind of power in *your* life?

Could it be that we're not prepared to take God at his word? The 'much, much more' of this verse is God saying, 'I can and I will fill you with my Spirit. I have the power to do that, but I need your love first.' Think about it. The first and greatest commandment is to love God with all your heart and soul and mind and strength. Have the faith to believe how crucial that is.

Continental

'I don't know how to love him,' you might protest. No you don't – but as in other relationships, such knowledge will grow as you spend time with Jesus.

Coffee

Love is a decision. Decide today to love God with all your heart, soul, mind and strength.

Orange Juice

Be kind and loving to each other, and forgive each other just as God forgave you in Christ.

EPHESIANS 4:32 NCV

THE COUNTERCULTURAL LIFE

The Big Breakfast

Life in the Spirit is a countercultural lifestyle. Oh yes, you'll find compassion and kindness in most people, especially when there's a major disaster. The human heart responds magnificently. It's the mark of the creator again.

The life we live through Jesus' power is altogether different. We don't turn it on and off as we choose. It flows from the life of God within us. We take no credit. Kindness, compassion, love for others, a patient spirit, a humble, forgiving heart free of envy and self-interest: these are the marks of the life lived in the power of the Spirit.

I was made to feel very ashamed the other day. A Christian colleague came to speak to me about a matter I considered very trivial. I was very busy at the time. I snapped her head off. Then I felt terrible. Her response to me was to offer to pray with me. I felt very small indeed. She was kind. She was living in the Spirit.

Continental

We're called to kindness and a forgiving heart. Anger is the oxygen that fuels the fire of unforgiveness. Submission to God's Spirit puts the fire out.

Coffee

Lord Jesus, help me. Pray for me, that I might become a God-filled person, not a me-filled one.